Stories
Grandma Never Told

Stories
Grandma Never Told

Portuguese Women
in California

Sue Fagalde Lick

Heyday Books
Berkeley, California

of this work may be reproduced or transmitted
ectronic or mechanical, including photocopying
ation storage or retrieval system, without
day Books.

l Warrin; page 92—Sirlin Photographers,
l 155— J.A. Freitas Library Collection, San
0—Mari Lyn Salvador; page 211—Michael
Jang, San Francisco; page 218—Doris Machado Van Scoy; all other photos—
Sue Fagalde Lick, who thanks the various people who generously shared their
family photographs with her.

Pages 121–123 reprinted with permission from the *Portuguese Heritage Journal*,
October 1993

Library of Congress Cataloging-in-Publication Data:
Lick, Sue Fagalde.
    Stories Grandma never told: Portuguese women in California / Sue Fagalde
Lick.
        p.   cm.
    Includes bibliographical references (p.   ).
    ISBN 1-890771-05-8 (pbk.)
    1. Portuguese American women—California—History. 2. Portuguese
American women—California—Biography. 3. Portuguese American women—
California—Social life and customs. 4. Portuguese American women—
California—Social conditions. 5. California—Ethnic relations. I. Title.
F870.P8L53   1998
979.4'00469'00922—dc21
[B]
                                                                        98-14247
                                                                             CIP

Cover Design: Rebecca LeGates
Interior Design/Typesetting: Rebecca LeGates
Editing: Julianna Fleming
Editorial Assistant: Simone Scott
Printing and Binding: Publishers Press, Salt Lake City

Front cover photo: Pauline Correia Stonehill
Back cover photo: Maree Simas Schlenker

Orders, inquiries, and correspondence should be addressed to:
Heyday Books
Box 9145, Berkeley, CA 94709
510/549-3564; Fax 510/549-1889
heyday@heydaybooks.com

Printed in the United States of America

10 9 8 7 6 5 4 3 2 1

Contents

Acknowledgments

A BOOK LIKE THIS would be impossible to write without help and encouragement from a lot of people. I must recognize the Portuguese women in my family whose lives inspired me to start this book in the first place. My mother, Elaine Avina Fagalde, grandmother, Anne Souza Avina, and great-grandmother, Anna Souza, are all part of me, and I am proud to share some of their stories. I thank Aunt Edna, Aunt Nellie, Aunt Genevieve, and the other women in my family who contributed memories and photographs.

I am also very grateful to the many Portuguese American women who did not know me yet were willing to open their hearts and tell me their stories, including the darker moments that might have been easier to keep private. I am awed that they were willing to take photographs off their walls and out of their albums and trust me with them.

I am grateful to the Portuguese organizations that provided moral support for my project and introduced me to some of the key players in the Portuguese community, to the Portuguese writers who paid their own money to publish their books and whose stories gave me a wealth of information to work with, and to all those who provided names of people for me to interview. I am grateful, too, to Joe Sanches and his Lusaweb, which linked me by computer with many wonderful Portuguese women.

I thank Malcolm Margolin and his staff at Heyday Books for their unending support and encouragement throughout the process of writing and editing.

I thank the Silvas, the Schroeders, and the Fagaldes for housing me on my interview trips to California. Finally, I must acknowledge the steady support of my husband, Fred Lick, who put up with late dinners, long absences, and little income for over a year because he believed in me and my book.

I thank God for making the whole thing possible.

Introduction

There is No Typical Portuguese Woman

IF I WERE ASKED to draw a portrait of a typical Portuguese American woman, I don't think I could draw just one picture. It would have to be a whole gallery full of different images.

One would be an old widow in black, an immigrant who speaks no English, rarely leaves her home except to go to church and the market, and devotes all her days to caring for her home and family. She carries a rosary wherever she goes and keeps up a regular dialogue with the Blessed Mother. Her days are punctuated with masses, novenas, and *promessas*. She cannot read or write in Portuguese or in English and has little to do with the world outside her door. She spends her days cooking, working in the garden, and crocheting when her arthritic hands allow. She came from the Azores early in this century, a fearful newlywed with a baby on the way, and she never went back.

Another portrait would show a woman in her sixties or seventies, dressed in stretch pants and flowered blouses, who spends her days cleaning and cooking, shopping, visiting with friends, or doing needlepoint. She worked at a cannery, a store, or an office until she married and had children. She learned Portuguese from her immigrant parents and never missed a festa or celebrated a holiday without sweet bread and *linguiça*. She grew up in the Portuguese community, but these days, she feels more American than Portuguese. Her husband is American, and her children understand some Portuguese but don't speak it. She rarely attends the festas now. Although she belongs to several lodges, she doesn't go to the meetings. She goes to church on Sundays, but only digs out her rosary beads for funerals. Although she knows how to cook Portuguese-style, she eats American food most of the time.

This woman may not have finished high school, but she had a lot more education than her parents did. Her dreams of a career were abandoned when her family needed her to quit school and help support the family. She was married before she was twenty-one and soon became a mother, but she doesn't regret the course her life has taken. She has never been to the old country but figures someday she and her husband might visit Portugal—after Hawaii.

A third portrait would be a younger woman who came from the Azores in the 1970s. Unlike her predecessors, she is educated and knew English fairly well when she arrived. Today she is a career woman, holding down a good job in government, education, or industry. But at home, she is a wife and mother, and her old-fashioned husband still expects her to manage all the housework and childcare. That means she gets up early to bake bread and make soup, and she stays up late to make sure everybody has clean clothes and lunch for tomorrow. She patronizes stores and other businesses run by Portuguese people, but she shuns the old-timers in the lodges as backwards and from another generation. While the earlier immigrants left Portugal believing they might never see their homeland or families again, this newer immigrant flies back every few years. She is becoming American, but in her heart she is still Portuguese.

Then there is the woman like me. My great-grandparents came here in the 1880s from Faial and Pico. Four generations have passed. My mother's ancestry is 100 percent Portuguese, but she married a man whose heritage is a combination of other nationalities—German,

French, Spanish, and Scottish. And I married a man who is German and English. My mother does not speak Portuguese, except for a few words and phrases, so she couldn't teach it to me. Her grandma, Anna Souza, one of those white-haired widows in black, spoke Portuguese to her, but she replied in English. Like her mother before her, my mother stayed home once she had children. She always wanted to go to college but never went. When my brother and I prodded her to go ahead and take a class or apply for a job, she said, "No, your father wouldn't like it."

I was the first woman in our branch of the Souza clan to graduate with a college degree and pursue employment that was not just a job but a career. My parents didn't understand; they had assumed I would become a wife and mother like my mom. I was also the first woman in my family to be divorced. And I'm the only one who never had children of her own.

I grew up American. Before I started doing research to write about the Portuguese culture, I didn't even know where the Azores were. I had never been to a *festa*, never tasted sopas, never danced the *chamarrita*. Oh, I heard about them occasionally, and we did sometimes have Portuguese beans and linguiça on special occasions, but the Portuguese culture was never part of my daily life, except in subtle ways. I started embroidering dishtowels and knitting sweaters when I was a little girl, and I still love needlework. I learned to cook, clean, and organize a household; I was well-trained to be a mother and homemaker. I lived with my parents until the day I was married. But my life has taken a different path since then.

Now, as I interview people or go to Portuguese functions, I feel a little bit set apart and afraid that at any minute people will find out I don't belong. I know that is not true. I have always been warmly welcomed by my fellow Portuguese, even though I learned the language at night school instead of from my family, and I'm not always sure what people are talking about when they mention particular Portuguese foods.

"You're still Portuguese," Mary Machado told me. I'm grateful for that. Then my non-Portuguese grandfather reminded me, "Don't forget, you're part German, too." That's true. And I'm proud of that side also.

There can be no one portrait of a Portuguese American woman, although many have things in common. Over the generations, the picture changes, as it has for women of all ethnic backgrounds. However, I have found the stereotype of the shy, homebound Portuguese woman—obedient to her husband, dedicated to her children, and afraid to venture out the front door—is far from universal.

This book has been a long time coming. I started working on it in 1989. I had previously published *The Iberian Americans*, a book for young adults about immigrants from Portugal, Spain, and the Basque region. In my research, I had discovered few books about the Portuguese and none about the women. In far too many scholarly books and articles, Portuguese women were barely mentioned, as if they didn't come to America, too.

I set out to fill the gap with a book about Portuguese women. My crusade took me to the Azores, Madeira, and Portugal, as well as into San Jose's Little Portugal neighborhood and Sacramento's Portuguese community. There, I struggled with the language barrier and the men who appeared to control every organization. I worked with the Cabrilho Cultural Center, Professor Heraldo Da Silva from San Jose State University, and the San Jose Historical Museum, seeking financial support and contacts, and ending up helping to preserve a culture that had been completely foreign to me only a few years before.

Most men seemed to feel that the women were not particularly interesting. "She's just a housewife," was the general attitude. Many of the women answered my requests for interviews the same way, saying they really didn't have anything important to contribute. They were wrong. Once I started asking questions, the floodgates opened, and the stories came pouring out.

I interviewed approximately sixty women. We met in their homes, at their businesses, in coffee shops, over the telephone, and on the Internet. All welcomed me like family. Many fed me and invited me to stay at their homes anytime. They also gave me names of other women to interview. With nearly a million Portuguese Americans living in California, there are far more women than I could possibly interview, but I still wish I could meet them all.

Some of the women I interviewed have died. My Aunt Nellie Souza McKee was one of them. Others have given birth, changed jobs, or retired. But I have captured them as they were then, and their histories remain the same.

I will always regret that I didn't ask my grandmother more questions about her family history, and that I don't remember my great-grandmother, who died when I was two years old. More of the original immigrants die every day. The stories of the few are present in the many, as well as the stories that Grandma never told.

A Note About Portuguese Names

Portuguese names, like those of many other nationalities, can be confusing. In my own family, we don't know whether my mother's maternal grandparents were Sousa or Souza. Great Grandma Anna Souza was a Souza both by birth and by marriage. Her husband, Manuel, had the same last name and was probably a cousin. However, both were illiterate and always signed their names with an X. Among their children, who grew up in California, some chose to spell Souza with a Z. Others preferred the S. Who is correct? Their birth certificates were burned in one of the Santa Clara Mission fires.

My mother's father spelled his last name Avina. Grandpa's sister, my Aunt Eva, said it was supposed to be Avila, and that's what she used until she married and took the all-American surname of Smith.

The same dilemma occurs in many Portuguese families. One brother may adopt his father's last name, the other his mother's. One may spell it Aires, another Ayres. Back in the small villages of Portugal a century ago, it didn't really matter. Mail was delivered and records were kept by first names.

When the Portuguese came to America, many of their names were changed, either by immigration authorities who couldn't spell the Portuguese version or immigrants hoping to sound less foreign. Ribeira became River, Barbeiro became Barber, Joaquim became Joe King. Maria switched to Mary, Antone called himself Tony, and Amelia changed her name to Nellie.

Confusing the issue further was the use of *alcunhas* or nicknames. In some villages, for example, there were so many Silvas they had to use another name to keep from getting mixed up. Almost every girl was named Maria, so most went by their middle names or nicknames to avoid confusion.

Middle names, given to every baby in America, were less common in Portugal. Eva Gomes was simply Eva Gomes, no middle name. Sometimes that middle spot was left to be filled by a confirmation name chosen when the child became an adult in the Catholic church. Others used their maiden names as their new middle names. In some cases, the name was extended with several branches of the family tree or the name of one's village tacked on to assure that everyone knew exactly which Maria Silva or Manuel Perreira one was talking about.

Certain names keep coming up. I interviewed two Mary Cabrals and two Pat Silvas. I have talked to Mary, Maria, Marie, and Maree. I have tried to use as many names as needed to keep the characters straight.

So is it Sousa or Souza? Whatever a person chooses is correct for that person. I have made every attempt to spell people's names the way they want them to be spelled.

Meet the Women Who Shared Their Stories

LISTED BELOW ARE some of the women who shared their stories with me. In a book of this sort, one gathers information from many sources, putting the pieces together like a giant jigsaw puzzle. Those I spoke to whose names do not appear here added smaller pieces, but they were just as important to the finished product.

First generation, born in Portugal

MARY AZEVEDO E MELO ALVES—Mary, who emigrated from Faial in 1910, was married to John, a barber. They had three sons. Mary was director of the choir at Five Wounds Church in San Jose for fifty years and was renowned in the Portuguese community for her singing ability and her generous hospitality, especially to newcomers from Portugal. She died in 1971 at age eighty-six. The San Jose Historical Museum and the San Jose branch of the American

Association of University Women named her as one of their Women of Distinction in 1996. Her son, Richard, and his wife, Kay, shared Mary's story.

DEOLINDA MARIA AVILA—Deolinda, fifty, left Faial in 1962. She and her husband, John, who comes from from Pico, live in Mountain View. They have two daughters. Deolinda is the author of *Foods of the Azores Islands.* She recently earned her AA degree in early childhood education and works as a teacher's aide in the Los Altos School District. She was on the board of the Mountain View IFES lodge for nine years.

MARY SOUZA CABRAL—Mary, ninety-four, a native of Pico, has lived in Sacramento most of her life. Her parents brought her to this country in 1908. She and her husband, the late Joe Cabral, had four children. In her younger days, Mary hosted a Portuguese radio show. She also performed in local plays, directed a Portuguese dance troupe, served as Portuguese chairwoman of the United Nations International dinners in Sacramento, and was active in the annual Camellia Festival. The Portuguese government awarded her the Medal of Merit of the Portuguese Communities in 1991.

MARIEL FEDRÍ—Mariel was born in Graciosa and came to the United States in 1980 to go to college. She earned a master's degree at San Jose State University and hopes someday to get her doctorate in Portuguese and Spanish linguistics. Now in her mid-thirties, she teaches Spanish at Ohlone College, does translation work, and moonlights as a rock and roll singer in the United States and the Azores. She and her son live in Fremont. She was born Mariel Melo, but legally changed her last name to Fedrí. As a performer, she is known simply as Mariel.

FATIMA LOPES—Fatima left her native São Miguel in 1968. Now fifty-five, she lives in Santa Clara with her husband, Emanuel, also from São Miguel. They have one daughter. Fatima is the former director of POSSO, the Portuguese Organization for Social Services and Opportunities. Illness forced her to leave POSSO, but she now volunteers at the SES Lodge in Santa Clara. She started a senior group there, organizes trips and parties, and helps the members with immigration and other legal problems. She and Emanuel are also active at St. Clare's Church and are coordinating the parish's "Renew" program in preparation for the millenium.

MARY P. MACHADO—Mary, who came from São Jorge in 1921, lives in San Jose. She and her husband, the late Joseph Machado, also an Azorean, had three children. Mary worked with her husband on a dairy for many years. In recent times, she worked as a receptionist at POSSO. She is eighty-three.

DELIA BETTENCOURT MENDES—Delia left her native Pico in 1966 at age nineteen, with her husband Ludovico. They lived in British Columbia for two years before moving to Sacramento. They have three daughters. Delia, fifty, is a cook at a middle school in Elk Grove. At home, she crochets and volunteers at church and for several Portuguese lodges.

AMY DE BEM MOODY—Amy, who was born in Pico, came to California in 1954 when she was eight years old. Her husband, Steve, is also of Portuguese descent. They have three children. Amy has worked for the city of San Jose for twenty-seven years and at fifty-two is looking forward to retirement in the year 2000. She plans to do volunteer work, golf, and become more active at her church. She is also eager to visit Pico again with her children, explore the United States, and see the rest of the world.

ZELIA ESCOBAR NAMAN—Zelia's family left Faial in 1959 when she was six months old. She graduated from Santa Clara University law school and practiced law in San Jose until she and her husband, Arthur, moved to Austin, Texas, in 1993. Zelia, thirty-nine, is now a member of the Texas bar association. She also does volunteer work and helps her husband in his accounting business.

MARY PASQUAL—Mary, a native of Faial, came to the United States in 1924, when she was three years old. She grew up in Los Banos, but has lived in Santa Clara all of her adult life. She is married to Ed, who is also Portuguese. They have two children. Mary, seventy-six, worked in her husband's upholstery shop and has been active in St. Clare's Church, the Young Ladies Institute, and other Portuguese lodges for over fifty years. She also belongs to the Portuguese Heritage Society, which oversees the Portuguese Museum in San Jose.

GUI SEQUEIRA—Gui was born in Pico. She came to the United States in 1968 at age twenty-one with her American-born husband, James. They have two grown daughters. She and James have been separated since 1988. A teacher in the Azores, Gui, fifty, now works as a computer operator for a Sacramento company that produces mailing lists. She is active in the Portuguese community and is secretary of Sacramento's Portuguese Historical and Cultural Society.

GORETTI SILVEIRA—Goretti, forty-five, was born in Graciosa, then moved to São Jorge. She left the Azores with her parents in 1966 when she was fourteen. She lives in San Jose. Goretti is the founder and director of Jardim Infantil Dom Dinis preschool. She has also been a high school teacher and until recently was principal of Five Wounds School. She is a partner in Bridge Publications.

NAZARIA SOARES—Nazaria, born in São Jorge, came to the United States in 1976 when she was fifteen. She and her husband, Alfonso, have one child and live in San Jose. A teacher and tutor in English and Portuguese, Nazaria, thirty-six, is taking classes for a new career in alternative medicine.

MARIA RAPOZO SYKORA—Maria was born in São Miguel and came to the United States with her family in 1960 when she was ten. She grew up in the Bay Area and attended Foothill and Ohlone colleges and Golden Gate University. She left a fourteen-year career with Wells Fargo Bank to travel the world with her husband, Karel, who was born in Czechoslovakia. They lived in Saudi Arabia for eight years, but now reside in Menlo Park, where Maria, forty-seven, is an office manager for CAR, Community Association for Rehabilitation, an agency that helps the mentally and physically disabled. They have one son.

MANUELA TORRES—Manuela, forty-seven, a native of Pico, moved to Canada with her family in 1968. She came to San Jose in 1986. She and her husband, Gualter, have two children. They own the Padaria Popular, a Portuguese bakery in the Little Portugal section of San Jose. For six years, she hosted a local access TV talk show, "A Nossa Gente." She also sells Amway products.

Second generation, daughters of immigrants

ELAINE ALMEIDA—Elaine's father is from continental Portugal, her mother from Pico. They both arrived in the United States in the early 1940s. Elaine, forty-four, is director of the Rancho Folclórico dance group and researches Portuguese songs and dances on her frequent trips to Portugal. She lives in San Pablo and works at her family's business, Adobe Liquors.

DONNA GOMES AUSTIN—Donna's maternal grandparents emigrated from São Miguel via Hawaii at the turn of the century. Her father came from Madeira. Donna, fifty-eight, grew up in Santa Clara and now lives in Cupertino. She and her husband, Scot, have twin daughters, Kristin and Nicole. Donna, a former nun, is a first-

and second-grade teacher for the San Jose Unified School District. She also has served on the Cupertino planning commission. She is avidly studying her Portuguese family's genealogy and is active in the Lusaweb conferences on the Internet.

MARIE SEQUEIRA BALSHOR—Marie's parents emigrated from continental Portugal in 1921. Marie, seventy, was born in Dixon. She and her husband, Al, have three children and live in the Pocket area of Sacramento. They work together at their family business, Balshor Florist. Marie helped write the story of her immigrant mother-in-law Graça Balshor's life in a book titled *Graça*.

LINDA AZEVEDO BRITO—Linda, twenty-three, grew up in Santa Clara. Her mother emigrated from Pico, and her father came from São Jorge, both in the 1960s. Linda and her husband, Paulo, live in Vacaville, and both dance with Rancho Folclórico Portugal, performing traditional dances from continental Portugal. She works as a medical assistant.

LUCILLE AND MARY ANN CABRAL—Lucille and Mary Ann, married to the Cabral brothers, live in the same Milpitas neighborhood. Mary Ann, sixty-two, is married to Herman and has three children. Lucille, seventy-two, and her husband, Marcelino, have five. Lucille's parents came from São Jorge in the 1920s. Mary Ann's father came from Terceira in 1914, her mother from São Jorge in 1910. Both grew up on ranches and worked in local canneries before they retired.

PAT SILVA CORBERA—Pat's mother came from Madeira in 1906, and her father, also Madeiran, arrived in 1913. She was born in Massachussets. Her family moved to San Diego when she was four. Her husband, Florentino (known as Tino), was born in Mexico. They have a daughter and a grandson. She worked at Breuner's furniture and then in management at Montgomery Ward. Pat, fifty-five, is active on the Internet, calling herself Papagaia, Portuguese for parrot.

BEA COSTA—Bea, seventy, was born in New Jersey, the daughter of immigrants from continental Portugal. Her father arrived in 1919. Her mother's family lived in Brazil before coming to the United States around 1920. Bea is married to Manuel, who was born in São Miguel. They have three children. Bea's family has operated Neto Sausage Factory in Santa Clara since 1948. Still working occasionally at Neto's, Bea is active in Santa Clara community groups and at St. Clare's Church.

CECILIA CARDOZA EMILIO—Cecilia, seventy-four, is a retired Spanish teacher living San Diego. Her father was born in Pico, her mother in Lisbon. Her maternal grandmother grew up in São Jorge. Both of her parents came to the United States in the early 1900s. Cecilia is active in the Portuguese Historical Center, Cabrillo Club, and Azorean Alliance. After attending a seminar in the Azores on Azorean folklore in 1987, she embarked on a year of research and wrote *Azorean Folk Customs*, now in its fifth printing.

LORRAINE FREITAS—Lorraine's parents both came from Madeira. Her father arrived first, in 1909. Her mother came seven years later, in 1916, with their son. Lorraine, eighty, worked seventeen years in the accounting department at FMC, twenty-three years in a furniture store, and several more years in a bicycle shop before her retirement. She enjoys golf, needlework, reading, and raising orchids.

MARIE DUTRA GAMBREL—Marie's father was born in Faial. He came to the United States in 1909. Her mother's parents left Faial in the 1890s. Marie, who has two sons, lives in Sacramento. She grew up on dairies in Sacramento, Newman, and Tracy. As an adult, she worked on dairies and ranches and spent twenty-five years as a waitress. In recent years, she has become active in Sacramento's Portuguese Historical and Cultural Society. Marie, seventy-seven, was one of the interviewers for *Portuguese Pioneers of the Sacramento Area*.

MARIA ROSA GIGLITTO—Maria's parents came from from Pico in the 1920s. She says she "snuck" in to the United States because her mother was pregnant with her when she sailed across the Atlantic. Mary and her husband, Frank, have two children. She has been a bilingual specialist and kindergarten teacher in the San Diego schools for many years. She is also president of San Diego's Portuguese Historical Center and president emeritus of the annual Cabrillo Festival. Maria, fifty-nine, has been honored by the Portuguese governnment for her work promoting the Portuguese culture.

EVA GOMES—Eva, the mother of Donna Gomes Austin, was born in Maui eighty-eight years ago. Her father left Madeira for Hawaii at the turn of the century, and her Portuguese American mother was born in Hawaii. The family moved to California in 1924. Eva has lived most of her life in Santa Clara. She and her late husband, Thomas, operated Gomes Market for many years. She is an active member of St. Clare's Church, exercises regularly, and helps her daughter with her genealogy research.

DOLORES SILVA GREENSLATE—Dolores, seventy-two, is the daughter of Portuguese immigrants. Her father left Pico in 1915. Her mother's father also came to America from Pico. Dolores and her husband, Norman, live in Sacramento and have one daughter. Dolores grew up on a ranch in the Pocket area of Sacramento. She is active in the Portuguese Historical and Cultural Society and was one of the interviewers for *Portuguese Pioneers of the Sacramento Area.*

NELLIE SOUZA MCKEE—Nellie's parents came from Faial in the late 1800s. She lived in Santa Clara all her life and was married to the late Oliver McKee. They had two sons. She worked in local stores in her younger days and was active in area lodges, including YLI, Druids, SPRSI, and SES, before her death in 1994 at age eighty-six.

MARY CABRAL O'REILLY—Mary, fifty-four, is the sister-in-law of Lucille and Mary Ann Cabral. Her father and maternal grandparents were born in São Miguel, and her mother grew up in Brazil. They arrived in the United States in the 1920s. Mary and her husband, Timothy, live in Monte Sereno and have two children. Mary works as a legal secretary for a law firm.

LOUISE PITTA POLSKY—Louise's father came from the Madeira islands in 1913. Her mother's parents were also from Madeira. Louise, fifty-eight, grew up in Monterey and now lives in Rancho Palos Verdes, near Long Beach. She and her late husband, Alan, had one daughter. Louise earned her bachelor's degree and teaching credential at Dominican College in San Rafael and worked as a math teacher.

JANE ROSE (OLIVEIRA)—Jane's father came from Lisbon, and her mother's parents emigrated from Faial. Jane, sixty, who has two children, is the former owner of Graceful Fitness health salon in Santa Clara and is active in the Unity Church.

VIRGINIA SILVEIRA—Virginia's parents both came from Pico, her mother in 1908, her father a few years later. She and her half-sister, Edna Sousa, live in separate houses on the same street in San Jose and have traveled all over the world together, including several trips to Portugal. Virginia, eighty-one, worked at a furniture store and Stanford University. She also worked in the accounting office at San Jose State for thirty years.

MARY NASCIMENTO SIMAS—Mary, the daughter of immigrants from São Jorge, lived in Santa Clara most of her life. Her father came from São Jorge in 1919. Her mother's family first left the same island in 1890, but got homesick and returned to the Azores. They eventually came back to the United States in 1910. Mary was married to Antone D. Simas and had eight children. She was very active in Portuguese lodges and social groups in Santa Clara County. She died in 1987 at age seventy-four.

EDNA SOUSA—Edna's parents came from Pico in 1908. She is the half-sister of Virginia Silveira and widow of the late Tony Sousa. She worked in the office at Food Machinery for sixteen years, then at the Pratt-Lowe cannery for thirty-two years. Edna is eighty-nine years old.

DOLORES FREITAS SPURGEON—Dolores's father left Madeira for the United States in 1902. Her mother was born in Hawaii to Madeiran immigrants. A Santa Clara resident, Dolores was married to the late John Spurgeon. She taught in the Jefferson School District, then was hired in the late 1930s for San Jose State University's new journalism department. She taught there until her retirement in 1975. Dolores, eighty-two, enjoys writing and traveling.

PAULINE CORREIA STONEHILL—Pauline's mother came from Terceira in 1908, her father from Faial in 1914. She and her husband, Len, live in San Jose and have two sons. Pauline worked as a high school and college teacher. She took up writing recently and told the story of her Portuguese family in the book *A Barrelful of Memories*. She and Len also sing and play in a recorder group. She is seventy-six.

KATHERINE VAZ—Katherine, forty-two, claims her Portuguese heritage from her father, who was born in Hayward, but spent his early childhood in Terceira, returning to California when he was seven. Her mother, who is of Irish descent, taught the family the Portuguese language and traditions. Katherine grew up in the East Bay and earned her master's degree in fine arts from UC Irvine. She is the author of *Saudade, Fado and Other Stories*, and *Mariana*, all based on the Portuguese experience. She is also a full-time associate professor of English at UC Davis. She and her husband, Michael Trudeau, live in Davis near the campus.

EDITH MATTOS WALTER—Edith's father was born in Pico and came to America in 1905. She also has Azorean roots in Graciosa on her mother's side. She is the widow of Tony Lewis, who was the son of Portuguese immigrants. She is now married to Joe Walter, who is not Portuguese but supports her Portuguese activities. She has two daughters. Edith did secretarial work for years and helped her first husband with his insurance business. At seventy-three, she is active at San Jose Historical Museum and on the board for the Portuguese museum in San Jose.

MARIE ISABEL SILVA WILSON—Marie's father is from São Jorge, and her mother is from Faial. Both came to the United States in the early 1900s when they were teenagers. Marie, who lives in San Lorenzo, has been active in the SPRSI women's lodge for more than fifty years. A widow, she has three children, six grandchildren, and four great-grandchildren. She is seventy-five.

Third generation, granddaughters of immigrants

NICOLE AUSTIN—Nicole's paternal grandfather came from Madeira, her maternal great-grandparents from São Miguel. Nicole, who is twenty-four and has a twin sister named Kristen, grew up in Cupertino. A graduate of San Jose State University, she is an elementary school teacher. She and Alex Delesio, a Brazilian of part-Portuguese descent, were married in December 1997 and will live in Brazil for a year before returning to California.

SYLVIA CARROLL—Sylvia, fifty-six, can trace her roots to São Jorge on her mother's side. She and her husband, Art, live in San Jose, and both volunteer at the American Youth Hostel in Saratoga. A retired teacher, Sylvia is active in the Portuguese Heritage Society and San Jose Historical Museum. She has one daughter.

ELAINE AVINA FAGALDE—Elaine's mother's parents emigrated from Faial, her father's parents from Pico. She and her husband, Clarence "Ed" Fagalde, live in San Jose. They have two children. Elaine, seventy, is a housewife, avid reader, and talented needleworker.

MARGIE FERNANDES—Margie's maternal grandparents came from São Miguel. She and her husband, Paul, who is also Portuguese, have five children. A former teacher, she began her career in city government as an aide to the city council and then to the mayor. Margie, fifty-one, was elected to the San Jose City Council in 1993.

PAULA PIMENTEL HOXIE—Paula, fifty-one, who lives with her husband, Phillip, in Camp Connell, has two children from her first marriage. Her paternal grandparents came from São Miguel and Flores. She recently became interested in her Portuguese roots and is active in Lusaweb. When not online, she delivers mail.

JUDY LEWIS JOHNSON—Judy, forty-one, is the daughter of Edith Walter and granddaughter of Pico native Rita Lewis. Her great-grandparents on her mother's side came from Graciosa. She and her husband, Robert, live in San Jose and have two children. Judy, who is a purchasing agent for the Oak Grove School District, has put on historical shows with her mother about their Portuguese ancestors.

PATRICIA BORBA MCDONALD—Patricia's maternal grandmother came from Terceira. Her father's ancestors are also Portuguese. She lives in San Jose and is married to Michael McDonald. They have four children. Patricia, fifty-five, is an artist and interior designer in the McDonald & Moore design firm. She designed most of the interiors for San Jose's Portuguese Museum.

MAREE CARMEN SIMAS SCHLENKER—Maree's grandparents on both sides were Azoreans, hailing from Pico and São Jorge. Maree and her husband, Ken, had three children. Before her retirement, she taught in the Campbell Union School District. Now sixty-three, she is active in San Jose's Portuguese Museum and lives in Roseville.

JOSEPHINE SILVA—Josephine, sixty-two, lives in Eureka. She is half Portuguese and half Italian. Her father's parents came from São Jorge. Her husband, John Cruz Silva, Jr., is also Portuguese, the son of immigrants from Terceira. They have three children. An artist, she paints watercolors and loves to make clothing, pillows, stuffed animals, and other things out of cloth.

DORIS MACHADO VAN SCOY—Doris's grandparents came from Faial and Pico. A Walnut Creek resident, she was married to the late Edgar Van Scoy, who was of Dutch ancestry. She has two children. Doris, eighty, a retired schoolteacher, told the story of her Azorean grandparents in her book *A Quest for the Story of Antonio and Maria*, which was self-published. Although she claims she is not a writer, she has been gathering material for future writing projects.

Fourth generation, great-granddaughters of immigrants

KRISTA HARPER—Krista's great-grandparents on her mother's side came from São Miguel. She completed her bachelor's degree in anthropology at UC Berkeley with a senior project on pregnancy and childbirth among Portuguese women. She went on to graduate school, earning scholarships and grants, including a Fulbright, to study in São Miguel and Hungary. After two years in Europe, Krista, twenty-seven, is back home in San Jose, finishing her dissertation and looking for teaching jobs.

CHERI MELLO—Cheri, thirty-three, traces her Portuguese roots to her great-grandfather, who came from São Miguel. A Los Angeles native, she is a junior high school teacher and moderator for the America Online genealogy forum. She lives in Torrance.

CRISTINA MENDONSA—Cristina, twenty-eight, is three-quarters Portuguese. Her father's grandparents came from Faial, and her maternal grandfather's family came from São Jorge. A weekday news anchor at KXTV-10, the ABC affiliate in Sacramento, she grew up in the Sacramento area and earned her degree in government/journalism at California State University, Sacramento. She and her husband, Jonathan Robinette, welcomed their first child, Kathryn Nicole, in August 1997.

Stories
Grandma Never Told

1

Let's Go to America!

RITA DASILVA was not the bride Frank Lewis was hoping for. When he left Faial for the United States, he had promised her sister Caroline that he would send for her as soon as he had enough money. Years passed without a word from Frank. Tired of waiting, Caroline emigrated on her own and married somebody else.

Unaware, Frank sent fifty dollars to pay his bride's way to the United States. Word came back that she was married. The only one left was the sister they called "Fat Rita." At 5 foot 10 inches tall and 200 pounds, the last unmarried sister was no beauty, but Frank had already sent the money, so he agreed that she should come.

The trip over was a horror for Rita. On the ship, she was constantly seasick and had trouble finding a private place to go to the bathroom. Her family had warned her not to eat the food on board because the ship was so dirty, so Rita lived on bits of bread and cheese she had brought from home. Rita spoke only Portuguese and had no one to talk to on her long journey. Her only company was a pocket-sized prayer book she had brought with her.

She left the ship in Boston, but she still had a long way to go. The tag on the little trunk bearing all her possessions said Frisco, USA. Actually, she was headed for Ventura, California, hundreds of miles south, but it was all the same to the Easterners. The only thing that got Rita across the country was the ticket she wore pinned to her coat that explained who she was and where she was going. When people questioned her, all she could do was hold out her ticket. Rita was afraid to eat on the train, too. Although the conductors were kind to her, when they offered her sandwiches, she thought they were trying to poison her. "Don't eat anything if you don't know what it is," she had been warned over and over. She kept shaking her head saying, "No, no, no." The mystified workers insisted, "It's good. Eat." But Rita kept saying no.

Strange food was not the only troubling part of the journey. The train stopped in Chicago before transferring to a line that would traverse the southern United States. The passengers weren't supposed to get off, but Rita desperately needed to go to the restroom. Clutching her satchel and walking carefully in the first pair of shoes she had ever owned, she hurried into the Chicago train depot. There, a black man playing the banjo "jumped out at her," she told her children later. "He was like a little monkey." To today's ears, she sounds horribly prejudiced, but Rita had never seen a black person before. She was so frightened that she wet her pants.

When she finally came out of the bathroom, still clutching her things for fear they would be stolen, Rita didn't know which way to go to find her train. She stood there crying, terrified she would be left behind. The train was about to roll when a conductor recognized the lost Portuguese girl and brought her back.

Surely her troubles would be over when she reached California, Rita thought, but she was in for another disappointment. This big, homely woman was met by a scrawny little man in a leather jacket. He was only 5 foot 6 and barely came up to her shoulder. He smoked and rode a motorcycle. She took one look at him and burst into tears. She did not want to marry this man. But she had no choice. He had paid for her to come, and she had to become his wife.

Rita, like many women in those days, did not marry for love, but for a home and stability in the United States. She arrived on February 2, 1917, and married Frank on April 16. Their first child was born the following February, and three more followed. "She kept telling me that she figured staying pregnant was the only way she could survive living with this man that she didn't like," said her granddaughter, Judy Lewis Johnson.

Rita had had a hard life in Faial. She had grown up barefoot in a little house with dirt floors, cooking over an open hearth, constantly sweeping and cleaning. She left school after only three years because her parents needed her help at home. In America, conditions were better, but the streets were certainly not "paved with gold" as so many immigrants had believed. For years, there was no furniture in the Lewises' house beyond a bed and a table. When others had refrigerators, Rita still had an icebox. Until her third child was born, she did not have a washing machine.

Her only daughter died at age twelve, and Rita never got over it. She clung to her sons. Two of the three lived with her until she died. Tony, the third son, left home to serve in World War II and got married after that. But he and his wife, Edith, lived nearby, and Rita remained devoted to her children and grandchildren. By the time Frank died, she had made her peace with him. In the tradition of Portuguese widows, she wore black for five years after he died.

Like most wives in those days, Rita did all of the household chores. She also worked on the ranch where she and Frank lived when she first arrived. Later, both did cannery work and shelled walnuts for extra money. There was always more work to do.

But Rita was proud and stubborn. She banded together with other immigrants and learned to read and write English soon after she arrived. She also became a U.S. citizen. A series of accidents left her with a stiff leg that made it difficult for her to walk, but she kept going. She volunteered many hours to help with church activities. She loved to cook and to garden and was still doing both until just before she died at age ninety-three.

Her daughter-in-law Edith Walter remembers Rita sitting in bed recovering from an injury and demanding to help with the food preparation. She sat in her bed peeling potatoes and cutting beans and kept watch over everything that went on in the kitchen.

Rita loved her garden. She could make a stick grow into a lush tree, her granddaughter Judy said. Even though her leg was stiff, Rita's friends and family would often arrive to find her "bent over with her hind end up, stooped over in her garden." She happily shared her plantings with the whole family, and Rita's flowers and vegetables now flourish in her children's and grandchildren's yards.

One of the biggest triumphs of Rita's life was sending for her brother and sister and their families. Like her, they came from Faial with only little packs and the clothing on their backs, seeking a new and better life in America, following in "Fat Rita's" ample footsteps.

THE STREETS OF AMERICA seemed to be made of mud, not gold, when ten-year-old Maria Sykora came to California with her family in 1960. Her father had owned a *taberna* in Ponta Delgada, São Miguel, the Azores' most metropolitan city, and was respected as a skilled chef. Here, he couldn't get a job washing dishes because he didn't speak English. Back home, Maria's mother had never needed a job outside their comfortable home. In America, she cleaned other people's houses.

They were used to being surrounded by family and friends. Now the parents and their two children didn't know anyone. "We were very lonely," Maria said. Even when they made friends, she discovered everyone was too busy to socialize the way they did in São Miguel.

They were also poor. "We didn't have Christmas the first two years," Maria said. Her family moved often as her father struggled to find work, first trying farming, then restaurant jobs, always turned away because he didn't speak English. Finally, he landed a maintenance position at a Los Altos Hills country club. When his employers found out he knew how to cook, he was promoted to an assistant position in the kitchen and stayed there for the next seventeen years.

The family's struggles were not over. By leaving the Azores, Maria's seventeen-year-old brother escaped the draft and the threat of having to fight with the Portuguese military in Angola. But in California, he found the changes so difficult that he ran away from home and began a life of constant trouble. His problems tore his parents apart, and they nearly divorced. Their relationship was never the same.

Maria, smart and mature for her years, saw education as her way out of the family's problems. "I knew I had to be assertive to get the education I needed to survive." Most Americans are not really aware of the cultural impact on youngsters who immigrate from other countries, Maria said. "The kids are never asked, 'Do you want to leave?'"

In São Miguel, Maria had gone to a Catholic girls' school and had taken piano and dance lessons. In California's public schools, she was academically far ahead of her peers, already versed in algebra and literature. She was used to being a good student, but now she had to start over in a new language. She also looked different from the other girls, still dressed in her formal Azorean clothes, while the other girls wore miniskirts and bell-bottoms, and wearing earrings in an era when American ten-year-olds did not have pierced ears.

The kids seemed so immature to her. In São Miguel, Maria had been taught to act like a "refined young lady." She knew which silverware to use at dinner, and she knew how a lady acted and spoke. In the midst of the casual sixties, she had been taught to address adults as sir or ma'am, never to call anyone "you," and never to address an adult by his or her first name. She was a young adult at ten while her classmates were still acting like tomboys or playing with their Barbie dolls.

She was also surprised to find herself surrounded by children of all races and nationalities. She had never met black or Asian people in São Miguel, where everyone is white. "I loved the diversity. I thought it was fascinating." She made friends with kids from many different countries. "Somehow I have a flair where I attract people," she said. "I have a good sense of humor."

But there were many challenges. Her mother never learned English, and her father spoke only a little, with a heavy accent. Neither parent had any formal schooling. They did not understand when Maria insisted she needed to do things with her peers after school to get ahead. When the principal came to their house to tell them Maria had been selected for a special summer school program, they refused to let her go. Maria loved modern dance and drama, but they would not let her stay after school for rehearsals and performances.

When Maria graduated from high school, her father, anxious to secure her future, announced that he had arranged a marriage for her with a young Portuguese man. Rather than argue with her father, Maria went to her prospective fiancé and told him that, although he was very nice, she was not interested in marrying him. She had other plans. Maria shocked her parents by moving into an apartment, enrolling in community college classes, and finding herself a part-time job. "I was determined I was going to make it," she said. She is grateful to Wells Fargo Bank for hiring her as a teller with only a high school education. She stayed with the bank for fourteen years, being promoted regularly. When she left, she was an internal auditor handling million-dollar construction loans.

Meanwhile, she earned her associate of arts degree by taking classes at Foothill and Ohlone community colleges and followed it with a certificate in real estate and business law from San Francisco's Golden Gate University. It was in San Francisco that Maria met her husband, Karel, a Czechoslovakian refugee who had fled his native country during the 1969 Russian invasion. A mechanical engineer specializing in power production, he had finished his education at San Jose State University.

Maria's parents opposed her plan to marry a non-Portuguese man. "I decided no one was going to tell me who I was going to marry," she said. Today, many years later, her widowed mother will not live with them because Karel is not Portuguese. She and Karel try to teach their twelve-year-old son to cherish both the Portuguese and Czechoslovakian cultures.

After their wedding, Maria left her job to travel the world following Karel's career. They went to China, Japan, Greece, and Australia and spent eight years in Saudi Arabia. Maria volunteered at the British school and socialized with the other wives of contract workers while her husband worked on the world's biggest power plant for the king of Saudi Arabia. She gave birth to their son there, and when he was a toddler, she started a day-care center, caring for children from all over the world.

Then Maria's father died. Her mother was aging and needed help, and it was time to come home. The Sykoras settled in Menlo Park. Maria now works as an office manager for CAR, Community Association for Rehabilitation, an agency that helps the mentally and physically disabled. She is a strong supporter of education, especially for Portuguese youth. She volunteers with the Luso American Education Foundation, which provides scholarships and educational programs for Portuguese Americans, and she would like to set up an exchange program so Portuguese youth could come here, and young Portuguese Americans like her son could go to Portugal to experience the language and culture there.

Although she is only in her forties, she has a lifetime of experiences to look back on. "I can't believe I was born on a tiny island in the middle of the ocean, and I've been to so many countries, and I've married a wonderful man who loves life and is so sensitive to human rights."

Asked if she would ever go back to live in São Miguel, Maria paused for a long time. "I don't know," she said finally. "I would like to have the best of both worlds." But she would not do to her son what her parents unwittingly did to her, pulling him away from his culture and his education. She would love to send him to the Azores for a year, but then she would bring him back to America, which is home for both of them now.

To the visitor, the Azores islands look like paradise. Why would anyone want to leave these lush islands where windmills turn lazily in the sun, where cows graze on endless green pastures bordered with hydrangeas as far as the eye can see, where generation after generation live peacefully in their whitewashed houses in villages where everyone knows and cares for each other?

For the thousands of Azoreans who emigrated to America, the virtues of their birthplace were limited. There was only so much land, not enough for everyone to have a piece of it. Schools were scarce, and an ambitious young man would find few career options beyond fishing and farming. Women had one viable choice: becoming wives and mothers.

Although they are part of Portugal, the Azores are 800 miles away from the mainland. The threat of forced military service for Portugal led many young men to leave before they were drafted at age eighteen. Azoreans also resented the totalitarian government that ruled Portugal throughout much of the twentieth century. Meanwhile, they kept hearing stories of the vast opportunities available in America.

Countless Azorean men and boys snuck aboard boats bound for the United States. Pauline Correia Stonehill's grandfather, Antonio Cotta, hid in a barrel for the long trip. His mother had bribed a sailor to smuggle him aboard. When he got to America, he went to work, earning enough money to return to the Azores and marry his village sweetheart. Five years later, they came back to the United States with their five-year-old daughter. This time, they rode with the other paying passengers.

In addition to the economic and political factors that spurred many Azoreans to emigrate in the late 1800s and early 1900s,

Pico as seen from the island of Faial, 1988

earthquakes and volcanic eruptions destroyed entire villages and sent their residents fleeing to America.

Portuguese immigrants also came from the Madeira and Cape Verde Islands, as well as from mainland Portugal, but the majority of Portuguese Americans today trace their roots to the nine Azores islands: Santa Maria, São Miguel, Terceira, Graciosa, Faial, São Jorge, Pico, Flores, and Corvo. These rugged volcanic islands, the section of Iberia closest to the United States, are approximately 2,000 miles east of New York.

Although the Portuguese have also emigrated to France, Great Britain, Canada, and other countries, America has long been seen as "the land of milk and honey," offering unlimited space and endless opportunity. With the Azores located on a straight line across the ocean from United States, the Portuguese were drawn across the water.

The Portuguese had been coming to America since the days of Prince Henry the Navigator in the fourteenth and fifteenth centuries and João Cabrilho (better known to Americans as Juan Cabrillo) in the sixteenth, but they began coming in large numbers with their families around 1870. The U.S. Bureau of Immigration reported that 14,082 Portuguese immigrated between 1871 and 1880; 16,978 from 1881–1890; 27,508 from 1891–1900; 69,149 from 1901–1910; and 108,927 from 1911–1920. The influx all but ceased with the imposition of strict immigration restrictions in 1920. From 1921 to 1959, only 480 Portuguese were allowed to enter the U.S. each year. Not only were the numbers limited, but many of the Portuguese immigrants could not pass the new literacy tests that were instituted.

Then in the 1950s, volcanos and earthquakes destroyed parts of the Azores, leaving many families homeless. In sympathy, the U.S. government eased the restrictions for Portuguese immigrants. The Azorean Refugee acts of 1958 and 1960 led to a new wave of Portuguese immigration. When quotas were eliminated in 1964, even more came.

The U.S. Immigration and Naturalization Service reported that, altogether, 434,000 Portuguese entered this country between 1820 and 1977. Of those, 37 percent arrived after 1958. The Portuguese have continued to come to America, although in smaller numbers as conditions have improved in their homeland. The totalitarian government was overthrown in 1974. In 1986, Portugal joined the European Community, which greatly improved their economy. Between 1986 and 1996, emigration from Portugal to the U.S. averaged 3,250 per year. The U.S. Immigration and Naturalization Service reported that 2,984 Portuguese persons came to this country in 1996.

Several sources have recently noted a new trend: people immigrating to the Azores instead of leaving it for somewhere else, but for many years, the wave of immigrants traveled in one direction—west to America.

Francis Rogers wrote in *Atlantic Islanders of the Azores and Madeira* that were it not for emigration, the islands would have been glutted with unemployed men as the population increased. As it turned out, so many people left during the peak emigration periods that the Azorean population went down. Today, there are more people of Azorean descent in California than on all nine islands. In 1996, the Azorean population was 240,000 while there were nearly one million Californians of Portuguese ancestry.

Traditionally, once an immigrant was established in America, he would send for his wife or his brothers or his entire family. They, in turn, would send for their loved ones. The Portuguese settled together in Massachusetts, Rhode Island, and California, helping each other and quietly working their way to prosperity.

Marie Sequeira's parents and older brother landed in Rhode Island in 1921. The family migration to America had started with her uncle John Sequeira, who had boarded a boat bound for New York several years earlier. When his beard and mustache froze in the cold weather the first winter, he decided to head for a warmer climate in California. Arriving in Gridley, illiterate and knowing no one, he got a job on the railroad and started making friends. When he had saved enough money, he sent for one of his brothers. When the two brothers had saved enough, they sent for the rest of the family, including Marie's parents, her older brother, and her uncle. The four brothers eventually went into a partnership on a dairy. After Marie's father died, the remaining brothers made her mother an equal partner in the business.

It was common for the men to go to America first while the women waited, sometimes for years, for a message telling them to come. In the late 1800s and early 1900s, women traveling alone were suspect. When they landed in America, they were held at the immigration stations until a man came to take responsibility for them.

But many women were as eager to come to America as their male counterparts. Writer Estellie Smith suggests in "The Portuguese Female Immigrant: The Marginal Man," published in *International Migration Review*, that in many families, the women were the ones to spur the move to America. "Data from one study revealed that for 85 percent of those interviewed, a female either instigated the

An Azorean woman, Terceira, 1990

move or gave it strong support; in only 15 percent of the cases was a move made despite her objections." Women, Smith noted, "are the ones who do the major share of the planning and arranging that may begin after the decision has been made, but prior to emigration. Most of the leg work (literally) is done by women."

Many of the nineteenth century emigrants left the Azores in secret. Art Coelho, a Montana writer, recalled that his maternal grandmother, Maria Cordeiro, couldn't tell her mother she was leaving for America. The only daughter, she plotted with her father and left in secret when she was seventeen. In the *Portuguese Heritage Journal*, Coelho wrote, "My grandmother knew better than to mention going to America. The first time she talked of leaving, at the age of six, her mother threw a wooden shoe at her from across the living room. And when she left Terceira, she left in the middle of the night in a horse cart, no one breathing a word to her mother.

"She never got to say goodbye to her. No farewell kiss for memory. And when the mother was finally told, she let out a painful shriek and took to her bed for months because of her grief."

Meanwhile, Maria sailed across the Atlantic and boarded a train for California. When she arrived, no one was waiting for her at the station. It was a hard way to start a new life.

FOR THE FIRST WAVE of immigrants, the trip was grueling. They came on whaling ships, cargo ships, and passenger ships, all of which were uncomfortable and took months to cross the Atlantic. There were months filled with seasickness, disease, hunger, and cold. Hundreds, mostly children, died of dysentery, influenza, tuberculosis, and other diseases. As they traveled across an endless sea, the women often pregnant or caring for young children, they feared that they would be turned back by the immigration authorities when they reached New York or Massachusetts.

Graça Balshor left mainland Portugal in 1911 with her husband, Arthur, and their four children aboard the ship *Ortisio*, headed for Hawaii, to work on the sugarcane plantations. During their six-month trip around the Horn, two of their children died in a measles epidemic on the ship. Conditions were primitive, and there were no medicines to save them. Graça, pregnant with her fifth child, arrived at their new home sick and depressed. The passengers were forced to remain in quarantine for thirty days because of the illness on board.

José Azevedo, Sylvia Carroll's grandfather, left São Jorge for America in 1873. His mother had died, but his stepmother sewed a pocket into José's coat and put in it one gold coin, all the money he brought with him. The journey was expected to take two weeks but actually went on for fifty-six days. The ship's crew ran out of food. The story goes that other ships twice tossed them packages of food. One package fell into the sea; the other contained only crackers. José resorted to eating shavings of wood off the boat to stay alive until he landed in New Bedford, eventually going on to Hayward, California.

Once on American soil, many immigrants boarded trains for their ultimate destination. They would travel across the countryside, unable to speak English, trusting that someone would let them know when they reached the destination written on the tags pinned to their coats.

The advent of the steamship eased the trip and cut the travel time across the ocean to less than two weeks. The steamers had better accommodations, which made the trip more comfortable and the spread of disease less likely. But it was still a momentous journey in which everything the immigrant had ever known was left behind. By 1890, most big U.S. cities had steamship agencies, where one could buy tickets for friends or relatives and send for them. The shipping companies began to advertise and offer extras to attract the immigrants onto their ships. One of those extras was train transportation from the East Coast to California. In 1902, steamship passage from Ponta Delgada, São Miguel, to the United States cost twenty-three dollars, a sum many of the immigrants could barely afford.

Mary Machado was seven when her family came to America in 1921. At that time, her parents had five children, and she was the oldest. It was a hard trip. Their ship, the *St. Vincent,* got stuck in the sand near Massachusetts, and they had to go ashore on smaller boats. They had taken two weeks to sail from Portugal to America, hitting a storm on the way. "My mother was almost dying. She was expecting my youngest brother. And with five kids, all crying, shut up in a room for two weeks, it was miserable."

From Massachusetts, Mary's family crossed the country on a train. With two berths for the kids to sleep in, her parents slept on chairs. "I don't know how they did it. Mother would say, 'Quiet. The devil only likes the mean kids, not the good ones.' We asked her what the devil looks like. She said, 'He's black. He's ugly.' We were all big eyes. One night, she puts us all to sleep, and the porter comes in and goes through the cars, and he's a black guy. We kids looked out through the drapes, and we saw this guy, and we started screaming, all five kids screaming, 'We saw the devil! He was here!' I'll never forget that. My mother never forgot it, either. She was sorry she ever told us that. We had never seen a black person before. To us, he was the devil."

During the train trip, Mary said, her father carried a chamber pot in a cloth bag. "We were scared to go to the toilet because we could see the railroad tracks passing."

Portuguese Pioneers of the Sacramento Area tells that Ellen Silva left Faial in 1904 at age eight. After three weeks in Rhode Island, she and her family boarded a train heading west. "At one point her mother spotted some fruit for sale, so her father got off the train to buy the fruit. Before he returned, the train began to move slowly forward. Ellen became frightened and thought she was going to lose her father. She began to scream and cry *'Pai, pai!'* The train conductor, speaking English, tried to comfort her, but she continued to call out in Portuguese. Her father ran, and the conductor helped him jump up into the train."

The decision to emigrate was irrevocable for most of the early immigrants. They were separated from family members who remained in Portugal forever. "They never went back, most of them; they couldn't afford to," said Aileen Alves Gage.

The immigrants' departure separated them from the family back home, but it also had an effect on future generations. In many cases, their children never knew their grandparents and soon lost touch with their ancestors' language and traditions.

Not every Portuguese immigrant family planned to stay in America forever. Some had every intention of working here a while, then returning to Portugal with their pockets full of money. Eva Gomes grew up in Maui. Her mother's ancestors had come from São Miguel, and her father was born in Madeira. Why come? "Survival. There was not much work over there." Like many Portuguese immigrants, Eva's family found work on sugar plantations in Hawaii. They were not done moving; the family eventually moved to California. But they always dreamed of going home.

Eva's daughter, Donna Gomes Austin, asked her grandmother why they came to America. "She said they always intended to make lots of money and go back. They grieved for the old country, longed for it, talked about how beautiful it was." But they never made it back.

When Mary Simas's mother, Rosa Gabriel, agreed to go to America and marry Antonio Nascimento, it seemed like a good thing to do. But not long after the birth of their first child, a son they named John, Rosa missed her family and home in São Jorge so much that she persuaded her husband to go back. Their return was short-lived. They had both seen far more opportunities in California. So they compromised; Rosa agreed to emigrate again if she could bring her family with her. The Gabriels and Nascimentos joined forces, working on dairies in San Bruno and Santa Clara, finally making California their permanent home in 1910.

IN MODERN TIMES, the trip has become much easier. While Rita Lewis spent weeks sailing from the Azores to New Bedford, today's immigrants come by airplane. In less than twenty-four hours, they are here. It can be an abrupt change.

Zelia Escobar Naman, who was born in Faial, was only six months old when her family immigrated in 1959 under the Azorean Refugee Act. Her mother was twenty-two and her father was thirty. Zelia, now an attorney in Santa Clara, said she doesn't think she would have the courage to leave her homeland the way her parents did. However, she added, it was almost bred into them to go to America. Everyone was doing it.

Like Zelia, Mary Pasqual doesn't remember much of her native Faial. She was only three years old when her parents came to the United States. Her father came first and sent for his wife and daughter when he had saved enough money to provide a house for them. Her parents never talked about why they left the Azores, Mary said. "You know, we never discussed those things with them. It's too bad that we didn't. I'm sure that my father wanted to better himself. He's the one that came to Los Banos and had a job. He worked with this fellow that had a dairy there."

Mary's father kept buying more property and more equipment. "My mother was always afraid we weren't going to make it." But her father did make it and was able to loan Mary and her husband, Ed, the money to buy their first house.

Manuela Torres was sixteen when she left the Azores. The whole family followed her father, as they had before, from one island to another, searching for financial independence. They emigrated to Canada in 1968. Manuela was the oldest of four children. They took her uncle along, too; he was in danger of being drafted into the

The Gomes family, c. 1913 (L to R: Frank Gomes, Cecilia Gomes Silva, Eva Gomes)

military. "The Portuguese always liked to emigrate. It's in our blood," she said.

Manuela's family found many Portuguese in Toronto. "The reason why we all moved to this country was because things were not good in Portugal," she said. "If they were good, we would have stayed there. The worst was not problems with money or land, but the opportunity to speak our own mind, to make decisions according to what we wanted."

After Canada, there was one more move for Manuela's family—to the United States. Manuela's parents went to California first; the weather in Toronto was too cold for them. Her father bought a bakery in San Jose for Manuela and her husband to run. The decision to leave what had become their home was a hard one for Manuela. "It was a rollercoaster of emotions for me. I didn't want to come, but my family was here."

Like Manuela, Delia Mendes started her westward journey in Canada. In 1966, at age nineteen, she left the island of Pico for British Columbia. Her father had died when she was thirteen, and her mother died when she was seventeen. By then, Delia was married to Ludovico Mendes and was already preparing to move. Her mother, who had been sick for four years before her death, approved of the decision. "She was relieved. She figured at least one of her children would go someplace to make money to help the other three," Delia said. She lived in Canada for two years before moving on to California, where most of her husband's family lived. His family had come to America because his mother was sick, and they could obtain better health care here.

Pauline Correia Stonehill's mother was only five when her parents decided to move permanently to the United States in 1908. The young girl, who had spent most of her life with her maternal grandparents, was heartbroken at having to leave them behind. "She practically sobbed all the way to America," Pauline said.

Decades later, Goretti Silveira, who was fourteen when her parents decided to emigrate to America in 1966, was eager to come to the United States. "It was either that or stay in the convent in the school back in Faial. Yeah, I wanted to come." However, she added, "After I came, I wanted to go back." Life was difficult for a teenager thrust into a new school where she had to master a new language to survive, Goretti said. As an adult, she wonders at her parents' decision to leave their homeland. "It's like everyone else is doing it. It's happening all around you. And you don't even think of some of the implications until they're happening to you right here."

The immigrants believed the opportunities in America justified the risks. "My great-grandparents really thought the streets were paved with gold," Cristina Mendonsa said. "I hear the stories of people leaving their parents behind, knowing they will never see them again. I can't imagine doing that now."

Nazaria Soares came to the United States when she was fifteen. Her parents' home in São Jorge had been destroyed by an earthquake before she was born. They lived a while at her aunt's house and, later, in Angola, where they had other family. But eventually they followed the thousands before them and came to California. Like most modern immigrants, Nazaria was educated. She went on to college to become a teacher. America has been good to her, she said.

IMMIGRANTS TO THE United States were often unhappy at first. Gui Sequeira was lonely when she arrived in Sacramento in 1968. Her in-laws were here, but her own family was back in Pico. Her brother and uncle had not come yet. Her American-born husband spoke only a little Portuguese, and she spoke only a little English. In Pico, she was educated and had a job as a teacher. Here, she had no work skills she could use. She did not know how to drive and had to adjust to everything being spread out. It took her four years to work up the courage to take her driver's test, she said. More than twenty-five years later, she still does not feel completely American.

The first impression of America was filled with disappointment for Delia Mendes. "It was nothing I expected," she said. "In the islands, the houses are built out of rock and cement, very big and tall, like two and three story houses. When I first got here, I thought the houses were like sheds. I thought I couldn't breathe in them because everything is so packed. I don't know how to explain it. At home, we opened the windows; we lived by the ocean, with fresh air, and here it is so different."

But today, Delia would never go back, except to visit. She and her husband recently remodeled their Sacramento home. Their three daughters are going to college and looking forward to high-paying jobs. The family has many friends, and they are active in their church and the Portuguese lodges. In many ways, the American dream has come true for them.

Mariel Fedrí came to the United States in 1980 seeking a better education than she could get back home in Graciosa. Beautiful as the islands are, she said, they are limited. Her brother complained that he couldn't drive more than two hours without running out of space. At first she told him he sounded crazy, but then she realized he was right. "You are enclosed there, especially on the smaller islands. You go on top of the mountain, and you see the sea around it, just like you are on top of a rock."

Here one can stretch out, literally and figuratively, said Mariel, who now has a master's degree and teaches at a community college in Fremont. "That's what I love about this country. There is no limit to what you can be if you want to. You can be anything you want. The sky's the limit."

Because the immigrants have tended to join family and friends already here, the Portuguese Americans are concentrated in Massachusetts, Rhode Island, and California. Many also landed in Hawaii, where they worked in the sugarcane fields before coming to the mainland. Although the first wave came as whalers and fishermen, beginning at the turn of the century, immigrants went to work on farms and dairies. The normal course was to work for one of their countrymen until they could buy land of their own. On the East Coast in the early 1900s, many Portuguese immigrants, especially women, also worked in factories. But their dream was to buy property and become self-sufficient.

The San Bruno home of Rosa Gabriel Nascimento, 1913 (L to R: Mary Gabriel Borba, Rosa's sister; Rosa Gabriel Nascimento; Mary Nascimento Simas, Rosa's daughter)

Mary Giglitto's father was one of many Azoreans who came to San Diego in the 1920s with dreams of starting a fishing business. He and his brothers bought an old boat that had previously been used to transport rum during Prohibition. In the years that followed, they built a fleet of six fishing boats, all with Portuguese names.

The tales of those who had come to America lured others to follow. Virginia Silveira said her mother heard stories from her aunt. "She went back (to Terceira) and they would cluster around, and she would regale them with tales of this metropolis called Salinas. They would just eat this stuff up. When my mother came to California and saw this little farm town called Salinas, she just couldn't believe it."

Although the streets were not "paved with gold," most of the immigrants stayed, helping each other, working hard, and shunning charity, passing their values and their dreams to the generations of Portuguese Americans that followed.

2

Portuguese Women Work So Hard

"MY MIDDLE NAME IS WORK," said seventy-seven-year-old Marie T. Gambrel. Standing tall at 4 foot 9, peering out of thick "cataract glasses" as she reminisced in her tiny Sacramento mobile home, she admitted she had had a hard life without a lot of lucky breaks. Yet she had an infectious laugh and was quick to note the good times as well as the bad.

Growing up on a dairy in Sacramento, Marie learned early that there was little time for play. The family got up at four a.m. to milk the cows, 365 days a year. Marie slogged through mud in the winter, washing the underside of the cows before they were milked. Her father was slow to get a milking machine; he didn't trust them. Everyone in the family had to help with the milking and care for the forty acres of alfalfa they grew to feed the cows. As the oldest of five children, Marie was also expected to help with the meals and take care of the younger children. A skilled seamstress, she not only made most of the family's clothes, but also sewed for the neighbors to earn extra money.

Marie's father, Manuel Dutra, was born in Faial. He came to America when he was nineteen to escape the extreme poverty at home. "A penny wasn't worth that much," Marie said, showing the tip of her little fingernail. Her father milked cows mornings and evenings and plowed fields in between until he had enough money to wed Mary Silva, a local girl whose parents came from Faial, and start his own dairy. The family moved from one site to another, leasing ranches in Sacramento, Patterson, and Tracy.

When Marie started school, she knew only Portuguese. "'In this house, we don't speak anything else but Portuguese,'" she said, imitating her father's stern voice. "When he used that tone of voice, we did it. My mother knew English, but she didn't teach it to us. She was too afraid of him because he was the boss."

As a result, Marie struggled in school. "Every recess I'd go behind the tree and cry," she said. Held back in second and sixth grades, she was sixteen by the time she graduated from eighth grade. Her parents refused to let her go on to high school, although her 4-H leader urged them to let her continue her education so she could develop her sewing skills into a career as an interior decorator. "The answer was always, 'No. We need her at home to work.'"

When her mother became pregnant a few years later with Marie's youngest brother, Gabriel, Marie cried for two weeks. "I couldn't get it out of my mind that she was going to die, that I would have to take care of that baby and the rest of the family, and I would never get married until maybe my father remarried. I figured I had the responsibility, that I had to take care of them."

In a way, World War II saved her from the tyranny of the ranch. Marie heard about jobs at a new quartermaster sub-depot in Tracy, very close to the ranch. Knowing her parents would not let her apply, she tried to sneak out. "I got to the porch, and here came my mother. My mother said, 'Where you going?' I said, 'I'm going to work, I got a job.' She said, 'Oh no, oh no.' I said, 'I'm going,' and I went.

"I said, hey, I'm twenty-two years old. And I was sick and tired of washing my brother's diapers. I was handling him so much he started calling me Mama. I said, 'Hey, I'm not your mama.' And so I went and they hired me." Her job in the cafeteria would provide training for her twenty-five-year career as a waitress.

When Marie was twenty-five, she married Dave Gambrel. Dave was from Kentucky, and he yearned to go back. It was there, living and working on a farm, that Marie, who already had one son, lost a daughter four-and-a-half months into her pregnancy. Hard physical labor caused her to miscarry, she believes. They couldn't afford to hire anyone to help, so she spent her days toiling in the garden and doing a lot of heavy lifting. "I lost her at home. I just put her in a little box." She asked the landlady if she could bury the baby in the family cemetery behind the house. "So she's there by a tree." Marie dashed away sudden tears at the memory.

The next year, the family came back to California, where she bore another son. When her sons were both in school, she started waitressing, continuing until ill health forced her to retire. Meanwhile, the marriage, always troubled, ended in divorce. "I had back luck in my marriage," she said. Her sons were already on their own. Marie returned to Sacramento alone and with no money. She arranged to stay with an ailing uncle in exchange for taking care of him. When he died, he left her his mobile home.

These days she lives on a tiny income with government assistance. Her first mobile home was destroyed when a drunk driver smashed his car into it. She used insurance money to buy her current home, which is small but cozy, filled with hand-me-down furniture from her family and memorabilia from the activities she enjoys with Sacramento's Portuguese Heritage and Cultural Society (PHCS). Using the skills she learned on the ranch, Marie stretches less than $700 a month to cover all her expenses and is proud to have no debts. "If I want to buy something, I know that I'm going to be able to pay it next month. If I don't, I don't get it." One way she saves money is by not having a car. A helper comes several times a week to clean her house and take her shopping or to doctors' appointments. Friends drive her to PHCS meetings and other activities.

She is tickled by the chance to enjoy her Portuguese heritage these days. The family attended *festas* when she was young, "but I wasn't no queen or anything like that. I always wanted to march, and they wouldn't let me." She giggled. "You know what? I've been doing my marching when I was in my old age." She pointed to the posters on her walls from the *festas* and camellia festivals in which she has been active. From her closet, she pulled out costumes she made: one red, green, and yellow, representing Portugal; the other navy blue and white, representing the Azores. She told her sons she wanted to be buried in the Azores costume.

Health problems plague her. Marie said she had ten major surgeries, including removal of ninety-eight gallstones. A bad back, heart problems, and asthma—so bad she had been hospitalized seven times in the past year-and-a-half—slow her down a little, but not much. "I don't think about it. I keep going," she said.

"DON'T WORK FOR ANYONE ELSE," Manuela Torres's father always said. "You never make any money that way."

Watching her bake 6,000 loaves of Portuguese sweet bread on a sweltering summer afternoon for the weekend's Holy Ghost festival, one might wonder if Manuela ever doubted the wisdom of her father's advice. It was because of him that she wound up owning a bakery. She was living in Canada, thriving in her career as a banker. She had come a long way since her family left her birthplace in Pico for Terceira, then moved to Toronto in 1968 when she was sixteen. She had dreamed of becoming a teacher, but she had to drop out of school when her mother became ill. So she earned her high school diploma through a bank program and rose to the management level, training new employees and helping the branch convert to computers. She was a workaholic, struggling to balance her children, husband, and work, but she liked it.

Her father decided Toronto was too cold and moved to California. He and his sons built a successful fish business in San

Jose from nothing. Then he looked for a business for Manuela and found a bakery for sale. She and her husband, Gualter, a São Miguel native, were happy in Canada, where she had her career, and he was busy making television commercials. But her father convinced Gualter to become partners with him in the bakery business. Unable to buck the will of both men, Manuela left banking and enrolled in bakery school.

In the banking world, she was known as Mary. After twenty years away from the Azores, she had become a Canadian citizen and conquered the English language. Suddenly, she was Manuela again, surrounded by immigrants as the proprietor of Padaria Popular in the Little Portugal section of San Jose. The fancy baking she learned in a Canadian cooking school was of less value than the family recipes her mother brought from the Azores. Everyone wanted typical Portuguese baked goods. Sweet bread became a specialty. Manuela supplied bread for local grocery stores, *festas*, and other community events. She baked cakes for weddings, birthdays, and baptisms.

Through the bakery, she has become involved in the Portuguese community, joining the Portuguese Chamber of Commerce and the Portuguese community center. Her shop, wedged between Sousa's Restaurant and Casa Nova Imports, is a meeting place for Portuguese immigrants, who sometimes spend more time talking than buying. The bakery stocks drinks, spices, candy, and other foods imported from Portugal. Azorean cassette tapes fill the display case by the cash register, and announcements of upcoming Portuguese events are taped to the door. Beyond the racks of plastic-wrapped sweet bread, one can hear Manuela's raspy voice as she talks non-stop to customers, vendors, and friends.

Few people can talk faster or go on longer than Manuela does. For several years, she put her conversational skills to work on a local access cable TV talk show called "Nossa Gente." Gualter was producer and director while Manuela went on the air for a half hour each week, interviewing people from the Portuguese community—one week a radio personality, the next an author, the next a school superintendent. She finally gave up the show, but she still has plenty to keep her busy.

In the midst of the Holy Ghost baking frenzy, Manuela dashes across town for an Amway meeting. Her whole family is involved in selling Amway cleaning products these days. At a huge meeting that fills the San Jose Civic Auditorium, she sits eagerly with her sister, mother, and uncle, listening to high-ranked Amway officers tell how they found financial independence and their listeners can, too. Manuela, whose brother Gilbert has already paid off his house with his earnings, listens to tapes, reads training manuals, and attends meetings. She is confident the hard work that made her a success in banking and has made her bakery thrive will enable her to graduate to something even better.

She and Gualter have a successful business, a nice house, healthy kids. But on those hot afternoons when she wears a dough-stained apron over her dress and her legs ache from standing over the breadboard or behind the cash register, she can still smile because she knows this is not going to last forever.

Manuela Torres's family has found the gold in the streets of California. One day, they are all going to be millionaires because they were not content to work for other people.

WORK COMES FIRST. From childhood, the older generations of Portuguese Americans learned that work was the most important thing, more important than school, recreation, or romance. It was essential that everyone contribute to the family's survival. As soon as they were old enough to work in the home or on the farm, they were given responsibilities, from making the soup for dinner to milking the cows at dawn.

That's how it was for many Portuguese American women. Back in the Azores, work centered around the home. It was a sign of a man's success that his wife could stay home, and it was a sign of his failure if she had to work. The ideal was to make the wife a *dona de casa*—lady of the house. Some hoped emigrating would give them the financial security to do that. But it often didn't work out that way. Women who had never worked outside the home, who had servants and extended families to help them in Portugal, found themselves taking jobs in America.

The work was very hard, and the women still had to do most of the chores at home—including helping their husbands and children adapt to the new culture—but their jobs also gave them a degree of independence they had not experienced before. Not only were they away from home and free from the dominance of their husbands for hours at a stretch, but they earned money for the first time in their lives. For many, that was a source of great pride.

The first immigrants from the Azores, with no education and little knowledge of the English language, did menial work. On the East Coast, they worked in textile mills, weaving and sewing all day to help support the families. Others became maids or cared for children. Some who were skilled with the needle became dressmakers.

Mary Lopes Perry worked in New Bedford factories after her marriage. After the family moved to California, the mother of four got a job at the Alta Laundry in Sacramento. She also worked as a seamstress and supplemented her income with dressmaking.

Patricia Borba McDonald's mother, Adeline Lawrence Borba, also did laundry. She earned money in Palo Alto by ironing clothes and cleaning houses for wealthy women. When she moved to Oakland, she worked part-time in a hospital laundry.

Before she came to California, Mary Cabral O'Reilly's mother worked in the mills in Rhode Island, then came home from her job and washed diapers. The women in her community worked out arrangements to take care of each other's children because they all needed to work.

On the West Coast, Portuguese immigrant women were most likely to find themselves working on a farm, behind a stove, or at a cannery—or sometimes all three at once. For the many Portuguese

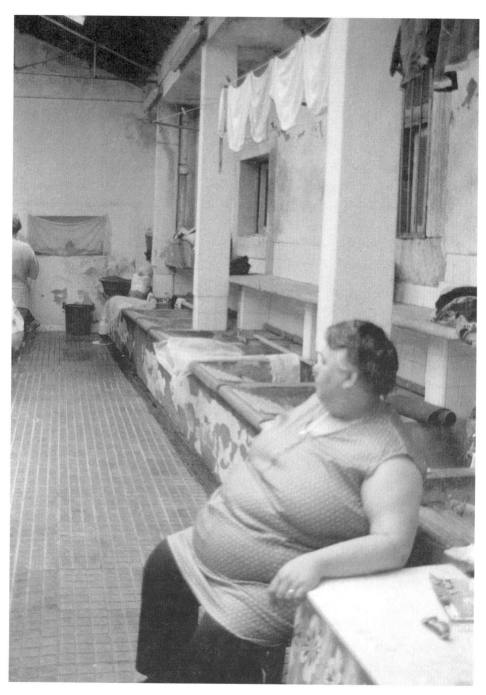

Woman doing laundry in Lisbon, Portugal, 1990

women who settled on California ranches, being female did not keep them from sharing the men's tough physical labor. In the Soto family in Sacramento, for example, the girls rode horseback, herded cattle, pitched hay, and fed the chickens and pigs. They also cooked, sewed, cleaned, and kept books.

When she came to California, Mary Cabral O'Reilly's mother worked on a dairy farm in addition to doing all her household chores. "My mother was like a hired hand," she said. "She worked right alongside my father and raised seven children, too." The typical Portuguese man wouldn't do any housework, she added.

Jane Rose grew up on a farm. Vacations were rare. "There's no such thing as vacations. There's no such thing as Easter. You work night and day, seven days a week." She and her mother fed the help three big meals a day. They would cook and wash dishes constantly. "I don't think my mother ever went anywhere. How could she?"

Minnie Perry Corey went from picking hops as a teenager to cooking for the men who worked on the *Argyle*, a Sacramento River dredge. Minnie would get up at four a.m. to start the day's cooking, making bread and pies and preparing three full meals, plus a midnight meal for the night crew. She also had to have snacks ready for the men in case they were hungry in-between. Her day didn't end until she cleaned up after the last meal.

From the *Argyle*, Minnie and her husband, John, went to labor on a ranch, John working with the horses and Minnie cooking for the hay press crew. She put together her meals in a portable cookhouse, which was sometimes moved while Minnie was cooking. Minnie went from the cookhouse to the cannery, working twenty-four seasons before she finally retired from a lifetime of cooking and canning.

Sylvia Carroll's grandmother Rose Lawrence Azevedo not only took care of the children, but cared for chickens, cows, pigs, and the garden. Her days started at four a.m. when she fired up the wood stove to make breakfast for her husband and children and the hired workers. She would barely finish breakfast before it was time to start lunch and then dinner, in those days before modern electronic appliances and instant food. In between, she made clothing and quilts for the whole family.

By the time she was thirteen, Marie Balshor was spending her summers working at an orange stand and car-hopping at a local eatery. She had always worked hard on the dairy where she lived, especially during World War II when men were scarce. "They would put me up on top of this horse-drawn cart, and they would stack the alfalfa, and I had to put it just right. I can always remember, you put it on the sides, you leave the middle. I was able to stack a pretty good stack of hay, and they were able to bring it in, and then they would chop it for the cows. But I had tremendous allergies and never knew what it was all about. One of the things I was allergic to was the alfalfa."

"My big job," Marie said, "was to clean the milk barn. I had boots up to here. I would take the you-know-what, fill the wheelbarrow up with it, and put it up on the chute. I fell in one time. I didn't suffocate, but I was pretty messy."

It was not unusual to take on several jobs at once. Marie's mother-in-law, Graça Balshor, for example, took in boarders, worked in the local cannery, and cooked and washed clothes for the hired hands at Sacramento-area prune ranches and asparagus farms—on top of raising twelve children.

During the Depression, another Sacramentan, Filomena Bothello, raised pigs, cows, and chickens; worked in the garden; baked bread; and made soap from pig lard and lye. In the summer, she worked all day packing fruit, then spent her evenings packing pears for another employer. *Portuguese Pioneers of the Sacramento Area* reports that it took eighteen years for Filomena and her husband, Antone Rose, to raise $5,000 to pay for their ranch.

Cannery work was one of the most common options for Portuguese women in California. In the early 1900s, when Santa Clara Valley was known for its fruit and vegetables rather than computers, thousands of Portuguese women joined other immigrants at the local canneries. Buses picked them up and took them to vast warehouses, where they worked twelve-hour days on their feet in sweltering heat, sorting, cutting, or canning tomatoes, apricots, peaches, and prunes. Pratt-Lowe, Duffy-Mott, Del Monte, Glorietta, F.G. Wool, Barron-Gray, Libby, Sunsweet, and other companies provided seasonal income much needed by the large Portuguese families struggling to get ahead. Mothers brought their sisters and daughters to work with them. The extra income helped some families send their children to college so they could have better jobs than their parents had.

In an article she titled "Reflections Within My Kaleidoscope," Mary Simas recalled working in a Chinese cannery in the Alviso area when she was only twelve years old. "A truck equipped with benches would travel around to the area's farms and pick up women to work. My mother and I worked together during the 'season.' The days often stretched out over a shift of up to twelve hours. Thankfully, the cannery season was relatively short."

Edith Walter worked in canneries during World War II. As a little girl, she had started cutting apricots even before she was old enough to handle a knife. She demonstrated how she held a cot in the palm of her hand, went to slice it with the sharp knife, and gashed her hand instead. She quickly learned a safer technique. "I got so I was the fastest cutter in the dryer. I cut twenty-one boxes a day, ten cents a box. I made two dollars and ten cents a day. That was from about eight in the morning 'til six at night."

They lived on Old Oakland Road at a place called Wayne Station, named for the train depot there. They cut cots and picked prunes. The whole family contracted to work in season. In the fall, they shelled walnuts for local orchards. After school, cracking walnuts took priority over homework—two boxes before supper. Then she would help her mother with dinner, and the whole family would work on walnuts around the table after dinner. It brought in much-needed money.

"My mother worked very hard," Edith said. "She worked in the canneries. In the summer, she worked cutting apricots at the dryer with me, and she picked prunes. When we got through, we went to Santa Cruz for a vacation, the whole family."

The work got better in subsequent generations. Like many Portuguese women, Deolinda Avila's mother worked in a cannery when the family first came to San Jose. It was hard work, but it lasted only a few months a year, providing extra cash without disrupting family life. Deolinda's mother spent twelve seasons in the cannery, but Deolinda decided after one day on a potato chip assembly line that she wanted to do something else. She took a nurse's aide course instead. In recent years, she has taken many other courses and now works part-time as a teacher's aide.

GROWING UP, many American women of Portuguese descent have found their career options limited by prejudice, finances, or circumstance. In some cases, their parents or husbands decided to leave Portugal just when they were about to start a new career. Others were forced to stay home and take care of the family when their parents were injured or died. And many never got the education they needed for the work they really wanted to do.

When Gui Sequeira came to the United States at age twenty-one, she had been working as a teacher in Pico. Here, despite her Azorean education and experience, she had no job skills. She could not work as a teacher without going back to school, but her first daughter was born a year after they were married. She gave birth to a second daughter four years later. Gui became a stay-at-home mom, taking care of her daughters and her nephews. When they were all old enough to go to school, she found a job as a computer operator at a company that produces mailing lists. These days, she wishes she had finished her education at an American college and continued her teaching career.

Mary Cabral O'Reilly, the youngest in her family, graduated from high school and went to work. "I brought home my paycheck and turned it over to them. Dad was working, and Mom was still working in the canneries, but it was not enough. At the time, I didn't think it was so bad." She was conscious of how hard her parents worked and wanted to help make things easier for them. Now she wishes she had gone to college but thinks she did the right thing. She has a good job as a legal secretary. At one time, she considered going to law school, but her children came along, and she's content where she is.

Her sister-in-law, Mary Ann Cabral, quit high school and started working at home when her mother became ill. She had other plans, but they fell by the wayside. "I always wanted to be a nurse, but I never got a chance to do it, so I figure, well, too late now."

Instead, she spent many years working in canneries, moving up to lab technician and quality control supervisor. She started at the bottom, she said. When she first applied for a cannery job, she lied about her age, saying she was eighteen when she was only fifteen. "We needed the money bad at that time. I've been working ever since. It was hard work. You worked ten to twelve hours a day, Saturdays and Sundays. When you had to have the money, you just had to do it. My mother had been sick for fifteen years." Before she retired, she worked from June to October. "I don't want to work year round. I worked enough as a kid. Now I want to take it easy, enjoy my grandkids."

Mary Ann's sister-in-law Lucille Cabral had different plans. "I wanted to be a hairdresser." During World War II, many of her friends headed for an out-of-town beauty college, but Lucille's overprotective parents wouldn't let her join them. "Of course, I was a girl; I could not leave town, I could not sleep alone over there. I told my mother, 'You should let me go.' I had a cousin up there, but I didn't get to go. I used to fix my mother-in-law's and everybody's hair. I had the talent to do it, but they didn't let me go. That was it. That was my career. I got married, had five kids."

Lucille worked in a cannery and a laundry. She also waited tables, but after her children were born, she had to quit. "I was paying more for babysitting than I was making."

Pat Silva Corbera was accepted to California State University, San Diego, but that was the year her parents decided to move north. Her mother hoped that the change in location would convince her fishermen sons to get out of that dangerous business. So Pat went to business school instead, studying accounting. A summer job at Breuner's furniture store in Oakland turned into a career in retail. She went on to Montgomery Ward, working twenty-two years in management, first as a personnel manager and then as an assistant service manager. Both jobs were traditionally held by men, she noted.

WHATEVER WORK THEY DID, the Portuguese women were proud of it. Bea Costa worked with her husband and father in the family's sausage business, which grew into a successful store in Santa Clara and a factory that today supplies much of the area's *linguiça*. As she was growing up, it was assumed Bea would stay in the business. She might have liked to do other things, she said. She was her high school class valedictorian and loved to read and write, but she never went to college.

After her husband retired, Bea stayed on at the store because she enjoyed it. "I like to be with the people. That's the fun part. It's a lot of work, but it's fun being with the people." Bea's son and two daughters have now taken over most of the business.

However hard Portuguese American women work in the United States, it's worse in the old country, Bea said. "Young girls fifteen and sixteen look like they're thirty or thirty-five. They get worn out." They work in the fields as well as at home. "The men in Portugal are kind-of like macho men. The women do everything, and the man just relaxes. I'm not saying they don't work, but they're done at a certain time, and the woman is never done. She can work in the fields and come home and do her other housework." Bea had hoped it had changed since the days when her family came over from mainland Portugal, but it was still the same when she went back to visit, she said.

Lorraine Freitas worked seventeen years in FMC Corporation's accounting department, being promoted to assistant supervisor, then worked in a furniture store for twenty-three years. She was also in the bicycle business. "I know how to repair tires," she boasted. She never married, but said, "I think I turned out all right."

Freitas said she sometimes wonders why the Portuguese have taken so long to advance in the work world. She thinks it's because they were too busy making a living. But the older generation began to see the value of education, and slowly Portuguese Americans have moved up.

Edith Walter wanted to be a beautician. She always did the family's and neighbors' hair. She graduated from high school at sixteen, having skipped some grades, and went to the Sullivan Beauty College. Her first customer had head lice, and she wouldn't touch her. She got an F and lost her ambition to be a hairdresser. Her next choice was secretarial work, so she went to Heald Business College and worked as a secretary during World War II. She loved to type. Later, she worked for State Farm Insurance and then for Federal Clothing Stores. When she got pregnant, she did typing at home, helping her husband with his insurance business.

Edna Sousa also did office work, sixteen years at FMC, then thirty-two years at the Pratt-Lowe cannery. She loved it, she said. Edna's sister, Virginia Silveira, earned a teaching credential but worked first in the credit department at a furniture store, then did accounting in the publishing section at Stanford University. She spent the last thirty years of her career in the San Jose State University accounting office. Independent all her life, she treasures her intelligence and abilities.

San Jose City Councilwoman Margie Fernandes's first big job was bearing and raising five children, but she was determined to get an education and contribute more to society. She became a teacher and started volunteering for various city groups. Soon she was working as a city council aide. At the same time, she taught school five mornings and four nights a week. Finally, she ran for city council herself. "Like all good Portuguese, I just always work hard, no matter what it is," Margie said.

Over the generations, Portuguese Americans' attitudes toward what types of work women can do have changed. At the same time, the families' hard work has paid off in a financial security that allows them to send the children to school for the education they never had themselves. However, today's Portuguese American professionals know that the older generation is slow to let go of old-fashioned attitudes.

Zelia Escobar Naman is a lawyer. She knew she wanted to practice law since she was a sophomore in high school. Many of her clients have been Portuguese, but she found the men didn't respect her as a female attorney. Even her own father found it hard to accept her professional status. When she graduated from law school, he had tears in his eyes. She learned that it wasn't because he was happy, but because "I would have to work for the rest of my life." She was unmarried, and he felt she was doomed to stay that way. He believed women should be nurses, teachers, or pursue other more "feminine" occupations that they could drop once they married and had children.

Among the newer immigrants, many have turned their dreams into reality. Nazaria Soares, for example, specializes in languages, teaching English to Portuguese and Portuguese to Americans. She loves her work, but since the birth of her son, she has become interested in the holistic health field and is considering a new career that could combine her fascination with acupuncture, herbs, and other nontraditional methods with more traditional health care. In the meantime, while her son is still young, she says motherhood is really her full-time job.

Goretti Silveira saw teaching as the best job opportunity for a woman. "The only woman that had a job at that time was my teacher, so she was my only role model."

For Goretti, who was fourteen when her family came to America, the move meant she had to go to work. In the Azores, those who went to college were usually able to devote all their time to their studies. Here, she had to work all through school, taking jobs at a laundry folding towels, babysitting, housekeeping, and working as a waitress at a pizza restaurant. "You wouldn't find that back there," she said. Goretti was still studying when she was offered a job as a teacher.

Louise Pitta Polsky also became a teacher. "I did everything my grandmother wanted my mother to do." Her grandmother had hoped Louise's mother would be a teacher and marry a doctor or a lawyer. She scolded her daughter for doing housework, saying it would ruin her hands. But she became a housewife anyway. Louise was the one who went to college, became a middle school math teacher, and married a doctor.

Mary Giglitto of San Diego is another teacher. Her immigrant parents valued education and not only sent their own children to college, but also set aside money for their grandchildren's education. Today, Mary, her two sisters, and her daughter are all teachers. One of her nieces is a nurse; another is a doctor. The daughter of a fisherman and a housewife, Mary applauds the opening of new career opportunities for their descendents.

Portuguese American women look back and admire their foremothers for their hard work. "When the women came here from the Azores, they really worked," Edna Sousa said. And they still do.

3

Portuguese Women Make the Best Wives

YOUNG PEOPLE TODAY don't appreciate all the good things they have, Mary Machado said from her receptionist's desk at the Portuguese community center in San Jose (POSSO). Mary, then seventy-five, remembered what it was like to have nothing. She was seven when her family came to California from São Jorge, seeking a better life. They set up a dairy in Benicia and went to work.

"Oh, it was a hell of a place," Mary recalled, speaking rapidly with a slight accent. "It was nothing but mosquitoes and rats." The oldest of seven children, Mary remembered that her mother was terrified that the rats would bite her little brother. "At night it was the rats, and in the daytime it was the mosquitoes. Oh, she really suffered with seven of us. She heated water on the stove to bathe. She'd make a bonfire in these old tin tubs, burning bay leaves to shoo the mosquitoes away. She couldn't stand it. We couldn't even go to school because we lived too far away, way in the mountains. When we came to San Jose, I think I started school when I was ten years old, ten or eleven. That was hard living then."

After the family moved to San Jose, working on another dairy, things got a little better, but they treasured every blessing that came their way, especially at Christmas. "Talk about hard living, we did it. But I want to tell you something, when we had a Christmas tree, that was a special occasion. To us, a Christmas tree decorated with popcorn and papers that we'd make, that was a beautiful thing." The gifts were likely to be only an orange or some other small thing, but Mary said, "We appreciated everything. The children today with so many beautiful things, they don't appreciate anything. Sometimes, I see a child with everything, I kind of feel sorry for that child. They usually are unhappy throughout their lives because they want more and more and more."

Mary had to drop out of school during the Depression. Her father was sick with heart trouble, and she and her mother both found jobs doing housework. They would purchase clothes for the younger children in the summer so that they would have something to wear when school started. They would also buy flour, sugar, and beets in 100-pound sacks and store them for the winter.

"There was no help of today's times, you know, no welfare or anything. I was making fifteen dollars a month doing housework. I gave my family all my checks except one dollar I would keep for myself in case I needed clothes. My mother would do the same thing. My father could not work, and there were nine people to support. You look back, and you see how much we have today, and that's why the old people, we can't see anything spoiling, something just thrown away. It's wasteful. For what we went through, to see that, to me it's a sin. Waste bothers me to death."

Mary met Joe Machado at Five Wounds Church. He introduced himself, saying he had seen her before in the neighborhood, and offered her a ride home. She said, "No, thank you" and took the trolley. "He might know me," she reasoned, "but maybe he was using a line, too." Joe kept asking her, and finally, the third time he offered her a ride, she said yes. A year later, when she was nineteen, they got married.

Over the years, in addition to housework, Mary worked in canneries and packing houses, packing mushrooms, cleaning beans, and doing odd jobs. When they got married, she and Joe went into the dairy business in the Central Valley town of Livingston and were in for more hard work. Mary used to help Joe in the alfalfa fields. "I could cut an equal amount of hay like he did. I would start a forty with him, and in the evening, we'd have eighty acres of alfalfa cut, him in one tractor, me in another."

Their daughter, Marie, took care of the housework while Mary worked in the fields. "We couldn't afford a man to do the work, so I did it with Joe. We leveled lands, plowed lands. I'd come in like a pile of dirt. My daughter had everything ready for us to eat. It was really great."

She sighed. "I was married to him for twenty-four years before he was killed." Joe was fatally injured in a tractor accident, leaving Mary with the dairy and three nearly-grown children. A widow for more than thirty years, she remembered her married life fondly. "It was a wonderful life when I was with him."

She treasures Joe's memory, sometimes listening to a tape recording he made years ago or looking at his old hat. "I gave everything of his away to all the boys, except I kept his hat because his hat would frame his face in my vision. He always wore that brown hat, and I could see him with that hat. So when I used to hear him, I would go get the hat. To me, it was just like I could almost feel his warmth."

Asked why she never remarried, Mary scoffed at the idea. "I'll tell you the reason why. You see, he was a great man, a wonderful father for his kids. I didn't want another man to come in and boss them around. And they would have to knock before they come into their mother's house, and I didn't want that. I want my kids to come to the door like they do today and yell, 'Hey, Ma, are you home?' So why should I go get pleasures just for my own self and make it miserable for my family? I had one man, that was good."

Mary worked at the Portuguese Community Center for more than a decade. She held on to the dairy for a while, but couldn't keep it up by herself. Her son wanted to take it over, she said, but she insisted he finish his education instead. All three of her kids got the education she never had, and today they are professionals with good jobs. Mary's grandchildren and great-grandchildren visit her often.

Looking back over the years, Mary was philosophical. "Right now I'm seventy-five. I've had a tough life and an easy life, and I've had great children. They're the best kids there ever was." She added after a minute of thought, "It's been an interesting life."

IN THE OLD DAYS, daughters in Portuguese immigrant families were cloistered at home, without the freedom that their all-American peers had. Today, that is changing as Portuguese girls in all but the strictest homes do everything their friends do. But the daughter still has strong ties to home and has to answer to parents, especially fathers, who retain their old-country ideas about what young women should and should not do.

The older generations remember being restrained by their protective parents, who expected their daughters to stay safe at home until they had husbands to watch over them. In his book, *Atlantic Islanders of the Azores and Madeiras*, Francis Rogers writes that, traditionally, young women in Portugal lived with their parents until they married. If they went away to school, their parents made arrangements with relatives, a convent, or other safe dwelling. There were no single-woman apartments.

Wherever unmarried women go, adds Rogers, tongues wag. "The system is particularly difficult on women of all ages but especially on adolescents. Females are constantly watched from behind the lace curtains of the windows facing the street and from many pews of the local church. Thus, in the fatal month of August 1939, I, at the age of twenty-four, could not walk down an Azorean town's main street with a forty-year-old spinster member of the family with whom I was living because. . . the expression used in Portugal is '*Faz mal* ' which may be translated as 'It looks bad.'"

"I was raised really strict like all Portuguese girls from the old country," said Bea Costa. "I couldn't go anywhere or do anything. My mother didn't let me go to school until I was seven. She was afraid that I would cross the street and get hit by a car." In their last year of high school, the students had senior getaway day. "All the kids went to New York—it was across the river. You think I could go? No. No way.

"Well, I went to one dance. You'll love this. I went to the school dance with a boy that lived upstairs from me. Like a brother. He said since we both loved to dance, why not join him? I said, 'My mother won't let me. You know my mother won't let me.' He said, 'I'll ask her.' So she said we could go. I nearly died. We got to the dance, she was there before we were, the only mother at the dance. I told her, 'I'll never go again.' I was so embarrassed. Mother said all the mothers should go. That's how strict it was."

The only extracurricular activity her parents let Bea join in high school was Civil Air Patrol. Her mother would walk her home afterward.

Dolores Freitas Spurgeon came up against this protectiveness when she was in college. She was editor of the school newspaper during her senior year. Her parents wouldn't let her go to the print shop at night to check the proofs. "They just didn't see any reason why any girl should be running around at night." She managed to get other staffers to do the job for her, but it was quite embarrassing.

Mary Pasqual shook her head at the idea of going on a date. "I never went out on any dates. If I went anyplace, the whole family practically had to go."

Mary Giglitto didn't date either. She attended an all-women's Catholic college and said, "The nuns were far more lenient than my parents." She met her husband while she was a student, but they didn't go out together until she had graduated and was working as a teacher.

Marie Gambrel was upset that her brother Manuel was allowed to go out on dates and to dances. "Us girls, we couldn't go. So every

Friday night when he'd go out, I'd just bawl." Once, she asked him to sneak her out with him, but he refused to do it.

Nellie McKee benefited from being the youngest of eight. "I was the baby." she said. "They kind of petted me a little bit. I got more leeway than any of the others."

She loved to dance. "I'd go like a nut as soon as I hit the door. I was dancing all night long. Oh God, I used to raise hell. I had guys coming out of my ears." Nellie's mother would tell her not to go out, but she would go anyway. After all, she was working. "I was so important. I was making two dollars a week."

Deolinda Avila, a generation younger, had some freedom here, but when her parents sent her back to the Azores to study, she stayed with her aunt and uncle and found things were different. When a friend invited her to go to the park to hear a band play, they wouldn't let her go. "I stood at the window listening to the music, and I cried and wished I was back in the United States."

Even here, Deolinda wasn't as free as her friends. She didn't date, which her daughters find hard to believe. She attended Portuguese dances at the IES hall in San Jose, but always went with other girls, never alone with a boy. Even after she and her husband were engaged, she got in trouble for going to a dance with him and his sister. "My mother found out and she was furious. I was twenty-one." Things have changed. Deolinda's daughters went to proms and dances like the other kids.

But for many Portuguese girls, the ties still bind. There was a terrible scene when Zelia Escobar Naman moved out of the family home after college without being married. It was almost scandalous. Single women didn't do that, her parents said. Worried about her, they called her every day until she had a husband to watch over her. However, Zelia is convinced that women gain strength from living on their own before they get married. Portuguese women who go straight from their parents' home to their husband's house miss an important stage in growing up, she said.

BACK IN THE AZORES a century ago, young women didn't have much say about who they married. Their parents selected their husbands. Courting was restricted to chaste chaperoned visits in the parlor and maybe a moonlit clandestine conversation through an open window.

"Once she is betrothed, the girl is kept under the watchful eye of family and neighbors, who gossip if she appears to show interest in any other boy. If for some reason, the engagement is broken, the gossip increases," Francis Rogers writes.

Marriage came as early as fourteen or fifteen for many girls, often to men who were much older. They usually married men from the same village who grew up with the same customs and beliefs. If they didn't share romantic love at the start, they developed affection and respect over time. In some families, an eighteen-year-old boy might ask for a fourteen-year-old girl's hand, then depart for four years of military service, leaving her at home, tied to him by the engagement ring on her left hand. The girl would bring to marriage her "hope chest" or "happiness trunk" (*baú de felicidade*), filled with linens she and her female relatives had embroidered, and other things collected for the home.

If one daughter became unavailable, the next in line married the chosen man. Francisca Emelia Dutra was married to John Soto after her older sister died waiting for Soto to summon her to join him in America. Francisca, only thirteen years old, made the trip instead, marrying a man twenty years her elder and bearing eighteen children. Throughout their marriage, as *Portuguese Pioneers of the Sacramento Area* tells, John called her *"menina"* or "little girl."

Sometimes marriage in the United States was almost as calculated. Patricia Borba McDonald's grandmother came to San Francisco with her sister, who was a mail-order bride. Both sisters were *fado* singers. Somehow, word of these two young lady singers got to Stockton where Patricia's grandfather-to-be was working on a big ranch. He got all dressed up and went to San Francisco with his mandolin. There, he met Patricia's grandmother. After they were married, he brought her to the ranch, where she became the cook for forty people, probably not the dream life she had envisioned.

Her show business career was effectively over, her singing confined to parties and *festas*. She had her first child, Adeline, when she was only sixteen.

Adeline grew up to become queen of the *festa* one year. Patricia's father saw her there and was smitten. For six years, he tried to court her, despite Adeline's parents' firm disapproval. "My dad was a hellraiser," Patricia said proudly. When the couple eventually got together, her grandfather refused to go to the wedding.

In the old country, everyone married in the Catholic church. To do otherwise was a sin. Maree Simas Schlenker found that out when she brought Ken Schlenker home. He was not Portuguese or even Catholic. Her mother didn't want him to come to the house, Maree said. Over the years, they made their peace, but it was a rocky start for Ken and his mother-in-law.

In America, the customs grew looser as the generations passed. Virginia Silveira, herself single all her life, said, "First of all, you were supposed to marry a Portuguese. Then they loosened it up that you must marry a Catholic. I think now if they're the same color..."

Nellie McKee, the self-proclaimed wild one of the Souza clan, was unusual in that she didn't grow up dreaming of a husband and family. "I had no idea of getting married. In fact, I didn't care to get married. I was too busy," she laughed. "Then everybody else began to get married, so I did, too." She insisted that her husband, Oliver, convert to Catholicism before she would marry him.

Goretti Silveira, who came to the United States as a teenager, met her husband when both worked together on a project for the Portuguese Organization for Social Services and Opportunities (POSSO). They were good friends long before their friendship turned to romance. "He was my first Portuguese boyfriend, too, here in the United States," Goretti said.

Were there others before him? "Yes, all kinds of nationalities," she laughed. She studied at the Monterey Institute of International Studies, which attracted students from all over the world. "The language you did not hear was English."

The wedding picture of Maree Simas Schlenker's parents, St. Clare's Church, Santa Clara, May 21, 1932 (L to R: Gertrude Perry Giboney, Evelyn Ligenfelter Nascimento, Antone D. Simas, Mary Nascimento Simas, Ethel Neves Lewis, Manuel Simas, Ida Nascimento Borba, and Eleanor Bersano Maguire)

Her parents never pressured her to seek someone of her own nationality. In fact, her mother discouraged it. "My mother used to tell me, 'Never marry a Portuguese man because you will never get along with a Portuguese man.'"

Marie Gambrel would have agreed with Goretti's mother. None of the five siblings in her family picked a Portuguese spouse. "I said, 'No, I'm not going to marry a Portuguese man because I had too much grief with my dad.'" The Portuguese men were simply too rigid, she said.

It was okay with Mary Giglitto's family that her husband was Sicilian instead of Portuguese. They liked him, and the Italian and

Portuguese people had a lot in common. However, Mary's mother warned her to never marry a fisherman. Her own fisherman husband was always absent. Mary followed her advice and married a man who owned a restaurant. Three years after their marriage, her husband, Frank, took up fishing and was soon doing it for a living.

Mary Cabral O'Reilly said she definitely felt her parents' disapproval when she and her younger brother both married Americans. It was so important that they be Catholic that her brother's wife converted.

Mary Ann Cabral, her sister-in-law, said her parents were opposed to her marrying a non-Portuguese man. "I used to go with an Italian boy, and my dad couldn't stand him. 'God, do you have to marry one of those guys?' he would say. I said, 'What's the difference?'" She was eventually engaged to marry a Portuguese man, but he was killed in Korea. Later, she met Herman, the Portuguese man who became her husband. Mary Ann's children didn't follow her example. "You can't choose for your kids. None of my children married Portuguese," she said.

Of the cousins descended from Anna Souza, Nellie McKee's mother, most of the women married men who were not Portuguese. In every case, their husbands converted to Catholicism. Their children have married men and women of every nationality, and no one has voiced any objection.

PORTUGUESE WOMEN make good wives, my mother, Elaine Avina Fagalde, always said. Raised to believe the husband is the absolute head of the family, girls traditionally apprenticed to their mothers to become good housewives, skilled in cooking, laundry, needlework, and housekeeping.

In Portugal, the old administrative code named the male as head of family. Men expected their wives to obey them. The 1976 Constitution changed things. That document affirms that "spouses have equal rights and duties with regard to civil and political capacity and the support and education of the children."

Even when men were officially heads of the family, many Portuguese would admit, if pressed, that the mother has always run the household, decorating the home, choosing the foods, directing the children's education, and conducting the family's social life.

Facing the challenges in America nudged many couples into more equal relationships. Both husband and wife needed jobs to help support the family. Earning her own money gave the wife a feeling of independence

Elaine Avina Fagalde's parents, Anne and Al Avina, on their wedding day, 1925

she wouldn't have known back in Portugal. And some women simply refused to be bullied.

"My husband always let me do what I wanted to do," said Mary Souza Cabral, who wasn't quite fourteen when she got married. "Some other husbands wouldn't want their wives to be like me, but he trusted me. We always got along fine. He was an awful good father and an awful good husband."

In modern times, Portuguese couples are more equal partners. "He's a good friend," Mary Pasqual said of Ed, her husband of fifty-eight years. She was nineteen when they got married, and she spent most of her life helping him in his upholstery business. "I worked in the cannery, which wasn't anything that I liked to do, but mostly I was home; then when we opened the business, I was the one that did all the dirty work, closing up and taking care of the books."

Mary is proud of Ed's art and the furniture he creates of wood and cloth, and he supports her many social activities. They enjoy traveling together. "My husband is very adventurous, too. If I tell him I want to do something, it's 'Okay, when shall we go?' He's always ready." She pointed to framed photographs Ed took on their travels. "He's been a lot of fun to live with."

Marie Balshor sees her fifty-year marriage to Al Balshor as a gift from God and a wonderful partnership. "I'm very blessed to have such a wonderful man," she said. They have worked together at the family flower shop since 1950. "We give very freely to each other. We're always trying to make each other happy. You know, he'll sneak home a flower—and we work with flowers all day. I have to say I'm very blessed."

Today it is more common for Portuguese American couples, like other Americans, to end their marriages with divorce. Many of Maria Sykora's classmates' parents divorced under the strain of adjusting to life in a new country. Her own parents' marriage was troubled for years, but they stayed together. Goretti Silveira and her husband were divorced recently. It was a good marriage and a good divorce, she said.

Gui Sequeira has been separated from her husband for nine years but refuses to file for divorce because her husband was the one who left the marriage. Her separation was a heavy emotional and financial blow. Gui has not been home to the Azores since it happened. She doesn't know how to face her family. They were married for twenty years, and she never expected the marriage to end. In the wake of her separation, she dropped out of her social activities for several years and still has not returned to the Catholic church in which she was raised and where she was very active when her children were young. She feels as if the church punishes women like her for something that is not their fault.

While Gui is still struggling to accept the end of her marriage, others, like Goretti, feel that as they become more Americanized, Portuguese couples join the national trend that sees one in every two marriages breaking up. And some, like Marie Gambrel, believe they can be happier alone than stuck in an unhappy marriage.

In the old days, there was no divorce. If the marriage failed, the couple separated. They could seek an annulment, but the process was costly and complicated.

Circumstance can provide unexpected independence for the Portuguese woman. In the old country, some of the strongest women are the widows. They dress in black and mourn their late husbands, but they enjoy a degree of freedom and respect not accorded to single women or wives. At last, they can do as they please.

Anna Souza, c. 1940

A protracted mourning period is common in Portugal, although the custom is fading in the United States. The death of one's husband traditionally called for the wives to wear black and restrict their activities for at least two years. Many widows never remarried. Remarriage is more readily accepted for males than females, Francis Rogers writes, partially because the family worries about what will happen to any money or property the widow inherited from her deceased husband.

Anna Souza was a widow for most of her adult life. Her husband, Manuel, died in his thirties of kidney disease, leaving her with seven children. She wore black until she died in her eighties. "He was the love of her life," said her granddaughter, Elaine Avina Fagalde.

A man wanted to marry Anna, her youngest daughter, Nellie McKee, added, but she declined the offer. Her only concession to the passing years was to add a bit of white to her black garb toward the end of her life. She played the loving matriarch. "Everybody loved her," Nellie said. "She had the grandest personality of anyone I ever knew."

After her husband died, Maria Sequeira wore the traditional black. With a friend's help, she boiled all her clothes, even her underwear, in black dye, and refused to wear any other color for several years. One day, there was a sale at one of the Sacramento department stores. Marie Balshor went to the store with her mother. To her surprise, she said, "My mother picked out the brightest dress she could find." Although she never remarried, Maria's official period of mourning was over.

Painful as it was, widowhood also offered freedom from the constraints of marriage, allowing a woman to handle her own money, to travel, and to work as she chose.

Sometimes having an absentee husband could yield the same benefits. Author Caroline Brettell studied the lives of Portuguese women whose husbands had left to work in other parts of the world. In the town of Santa Eulalia de Lanhese, she found women working in the fields, selling oxen at the market, spraying vines, and doing other traditionally male tasks. Many were spinsters, never married because of the shortage of men. They disdained marriage, preferring their independence. Brettell quoted a popular saying, "When I was single, I used ribbons and ties; now that I am married, I have tears in my eyes." Another saying went, "When I married and entrapped myself, I exchanged silver for copper. I bartered my freedom for money which does not flow."

Because the sons were gone, daughters cared for their aging in-laws and inherited their property. Unmarried women and *viúvas dos vivos* (widows of the living) bonded together. While some lived with their parents, many had their own homes and were recognized as heads of households. Others decided not to wait anymore and went after their missing husbands.

NOT ONLY ARE Portuguese women good wives, but they are also good mothers. Bred into them generation after generation is the necessity to place their families above all else.

A century ago, it was not uncommon for a Portuguese family to have ten or more children. Birth control was unavailable and forbidden by the Catholic church. In addition, because many babies and children died before they reached adulthood, having more offspring increased the odds of ending up with some surviving. More children meant more hands to help with the work. Still, descendants wonder how their foremothers found the strength to raise so many children.

In her thesis, *The Portuguese in America,* Sandra Wolforth cites the prevailing viewpoint in the early 1900s that "the normal state of married Portuguese women of good health...is almost continuous pregnancy and childbearing, with those under age thirty bearing a child each year and those over age thirty, a child every two to three years."

Francis Rogers echoes her words: "After the wedding, female members of the clan await the first baby. As a matter of fact, they tend to persecute the bride on this score, as if constantly to remind her that the church preaches no birth control."

Gui Sequeira changed her mind about that birth control policy after her first daughter was born only a year after she was married. Before her marriage, she had been strongly opposed to using contraceptives. "I changed my tune," she admitted. It was four years before she completed her family with another daughter.

Rosa Soares, whose story is told in *Portuguese Pioneers of the Sacramento Area,* lost more children than she kept. She was a fragile woman with an unknown blood problem, losing several infant children before a son and a daughter survived. Then the girl drowned in a tragic accident. Rosa devoted all her efforts to her surviving child to the point where he was considered spoiled by others in the neighborhood.

Children were traditionally the woman's responsibility. If she did have a job, she was the one to come home to care for an ill child.

Childcare was too costly, so those who needed to work would alternate shifts with their husbands. In many cases, older children, friends, or relatives helped with childcare. However, as Louise Lampshere reported in "Working Women and Family Strategies: Portuguese and Colombian Women in a New England Community," it was felt that mothers were the best ones to care for children. "One woman said, 'There's always something missing when a mother isn't at home.'"

Back in Portugal, it was common for extended families to live together in the same house or at least in the same village. Grandparents, aunts, sisters-in-law, cousins, and others were around to help each other with childcare, housework, and other needs. Many of the immigrants found this missing when they came to America. Their older relatives rarely left Portugal. The young parents had only themselves to rely on. Wolforth writes, "It was a fortunate family indeed which had an unemployed maiden aunt or grandmother in residence to help care for the children."

Rose Lawrence was the second wife of José Azevedo. With his first wife, he had fathered eight children who lived and one that had died. "Imagine having eight children in ten years," whispered their granddaughter Sylvia Carroll. Rose, who was twenty-one years younger than her husband, took on a ready-made family. She discovered that in the three years José was without a wife, he had neglected things, including the children's clothing and their education. Each of the girls had only one dress. She demanded that they go to Hayward to get cloth to make more and set out to outfit her new daughters properly. She also decreed that her stepchildren would learn English. Rose and José had six more children, the youngest of whom was Sylvia's mother. Rose's stepchildren soon grew up and had children of their own. Many brought their children home to Grandma, especially if they were sickly or troubled. "It seemed like there were always kids going there for the summer," Sylvia said.

Mary Ann and Lucille Cabral of Milpitas worked over the years, but they believe in strong family values, which they passed on to their children. Her parents were strict, Mary Ann said. She tried to raise her kids the same way. "I was very firm with them, and I was glad I was." Now her children are experiencing the same challenges with their children that she faced with them. "I think being family-oriented, you can do a lot with your kids. If you don't care, they're going to stray. We always did things with the family. To this day, we still do. When I have family things, everybody's included."

Lucille said she tells her children that when the parents are gone they will be glad they spent time together. "I tell my kids, we're all here on borrowed time. I hope you continue what we have continued, because as you grow older, you're going to need each other a lot more because your kids are gonna be gone, and you're gonna need your brothers and sisters." Her own children remain close, she said, thanks to their upbringing.

While the mother did most of the work at home, the father was considered the boss, and the children respected him. "All he had to do was look at us and we'd sit up straight," Edith Walter recalled. "What he said went." When they needed to ask him something, the children talked to their mother first. "Not that I was scared of him, but it seemed like that was the natural order."

"Dad was the one who set the pace. If he wanted the radio on, okay. If he didn't want the radio on, the radio did not go on. And when it came time to go to bed, it was lights out, it's bedtime, everybody in bed."

Many modern Portuguese mothers find themselves working and trying to do everything at home. San Jose councilmember Margie Fernandes married young and had five children. Raising them became her full-time job, but she always wanted to finish her education and went back to school part-time when the older children were in their teens. Gradually, some of the burden of childcare and home chores was transferred to her husband, Paul.

Margie said she doesn't feel guilty being at work instead of at home because her husband takes good care of the kids. "I think the Portuguese values have stuck with us. Neither one of us have huge egos that we have to deal with on a regular basis. We just work hard and care about the kids."

Manuela Torres remembers the sacrifices she made to have a career and be a mother to her two children at the same time. "If you ask people what they want, what they would do with extra time, they need time with their family," she said. "Pretty soon time is going to be one of the most important acquisitions that anybody has. For women these days, they want to come home and be with their kids."

It's possible to combine children and a career, Manuela added. She did. She worked in a bank when they were young. But a working mother misses the best years of her children's lives. A babysitter or mother-in-law sees them instead, she said.

Those not blessed with children have their own burdens to carry. Goretti Silveira said she and her husband tried to have children and were unable. They considered adopting, but, she said, "That's not the thing to do among the Portuguese. Everyone—my parents, my in-laws—said, 'Not somebody else's kid, no.'" Now in her forties, she said, "I think my teaching kind of takes care of that part."

4

The Man is Not the Boss Anymore

 MARIE SEQUEIRA couldn't go to business college in the metropolis of Sacramento until her family found a suitable place for her to stay. But no lodging was good enough until her mother's friend Graça Balshor invited Marie to stay at her house. There was one condition: The teenager would have to share a bed with Graça because all the others were taken. Years later, Marie would joke that she slept with her husband's mother before she slept with him.

On the first day of school, Graça took her to the bus stop. "From that moment on, she was my friend. She just guided me." Although Graça has been dead for more than twenty years, Marie still chokes up with tears as she remembers the kindness of her mother-in-law and best friend. Graça's portrait dominates the Balshor living room, surrounded by Marie's vast collection of dolls and bric-a-brac.

Graça had endured a hard life and had every right to be bitter, but she held on to a faith that God would never give her more trouble than she could bear. "She took more than ten people could,"

Graça Balshor, 1972, photographed by Ted Sirlin

Marie said. Her philosophy was, "I'll still be here to take what He has to give me."

Graça had given birth to twelve children, but only five survived to adulthood. Two died on the ship from Portugal to Hawaii, one died of a sudden illness in Hawaii, one died of diphtheria in California, one was shot in a fight in Sacramento, one died in World War II, and her last baby died shortly after birth. Her husband, twenty-one years older than Graça, died at age sixty-four, leaving her with the youngest children to raise alone. Back-breaking work and constant poverty dogged her in Portugal, Hawaii, and California. At an age when most women gave up hard physical labor, she was still scratching together a living, working in canneries and picking prunes and asparagus around the Sacramento area.

She also served as a midwife, helping birth approximately sixty-five babies. Neighbors knew that when Graça Balshor walked quickly down the street with her apron on, a baby was coming.

"She taught me so much of life," Marie said. "'You can't depend on anybody else,' she would say. 'If there's something to do, no matter how it happens, no matter what the outcome, do it.'"

When Marie moved in with her, the other two rooms were occupied by a divorced daughter and Graça's youngest son, Albert. Although Marie had a boyfriend in Dixon and had never gotten along with Al when they were kids, romance blossomed in the Balshor household. One weekend when she didn't go to Dixon, they went out and Al asked her to dance. "Next thing I knew, he kissed me on the cheek, and that was it, that's all it took. So we got married on January 1, 1948."

All three of Marie and Al Balshor's children were born in Graça's house. The daughter slept with Graça, and the youngest son slept in the dining room. The Balshors opened a flower shop in 1950 and finally built a home of their own in the area along the Sacramento River known as the Pocket. It was hard to move out of Graça's house after living together for so long. "But you know, we went with her blessings. She knew our life had to go on. She loved this house. She loved me, and I loved her. We were the best of friends."

Maria Sequeira, 1952

Marie had grown up in two shacks put together on a ranch in Dixon, then shared Graça's house. She was amazed at all the space in her new house. "Gosh, when we came here and we had this big house, it was overwhelming, but it was really neat." Graça would visit often, but was never comfortable just sitting and visiting. "Grandma would say, 'You got something for me to do?' It got to the point if there was nothing for her to do, she'd go right home, so I'd always have a pile of clothes on a chair for her to fold, or occasionally I'd leave dishes in the sink. Sometimes she'd get disgusted and say, 'My God, don't you do anything?'" But it wasn't a criticism; the two women understood each other.

Graça was still friends with Marie's mother, Maria, who she always called Mrs. Sequeira. Maria Sequeira had had her share of hard knocks, too. Like Graça's husband, her husband died young, leaving Maria with a three-year-old daughter and a ten-year-old son to raise alone. Her husband had shared the dairy business with his three brothers. When he and one of the brothers died within two weeks of each other, Maria started packing, figuring her only choice was to take her children back to Portugal. But her brother-in-law stopped her. He told her he had promised her husband to take care of his wife and kids. She would be an equal partner in the ranch. In exchange, she would handle the cooking, cleaning, and clothing. "You never have to work in the fields," he said.

Marie's mother lived the rest of her life on the farm with her two bachelor brothers-in-law. "Wasn't that beautiful? It wasn't the way it was in the old country, but this is what he promised her," Marie said.

Marie admired her mother with her blue-green eyes, salt and pepper hair, high cheekbones, and rosy cheeks. "She really looked like a little Dutch lady." When she walked into a room, people noticed her; she had a presence. Maria Sequeira was slender and dignified and never went out without her corset on. "My mother was a great influence on me."

The Sequeiras and the Balshors seemed fated to be together. Before Marie was born, her mother had had another daughter, who was stillborn. As an adult, Marie went hunting for where her sister had been buried and was amazed to find her in an unmarked grave near the Balshor family plots. "I got so moved with that. It was so close. It was destiny that we should be together."

When a mutual friend first brought Mrs. Balshor to meet Mrs. Sequeira, Marie said, "Immediately my mother liked her. There was just a wonderful magic between the two of them." The Balshors would come over for the annual butchering of the pig, and Graça sent Al to the Sequeiras to experience farm life during the summer. Maria would give Graça chickens, milk, and vegetables to take home. She would take her children to visit the Balshors in the "big city."

Graça was the one who got a hot water heater installed in Maria's home. Maria had hesitated to ask her brothers-in-law. All her life, she had heated water on the stove. Graça waited until Maria was away for a few days and ordered the men to install the hot water heater.

Marie's mother preceded Graça in death. Both women had planned to go to Portugal together, but Graça had to change her plans. Maria went with friends instead. Her last letter to her daughter told her it was a wonderful experience. "The whole village came out for her. She had left in 1921 and this was 1952." One day shy of her fifty-eighth birthday, Maria died in her home village of Penela da Beira Alta. "She went home to die," Marie said. "I always felt that God was with her."

Graça went to Portugal for several months after Marie's mother died, then she returned to Sacramento, where she and Marie became closer than ever.

Being Graça's daughter-in-law and close friend, Marie knew the story of her life. As Graça's ninetieth birthday approached, she decided to capture the older woman's memories in a book. A friend, Deanna Prisco, offered to write it, using the information Marie gave her. They had 500 copies printed and gave them out at Graça's birthday party that year. Each family got a book; the remainder were given to others who knew Graça. It was a glorious occasion. "She was queen that day, and she got up and she talked."

Sacramento photographer Ted Sirlin had taken Graça's portrait for the book and was so pleased with it that he showed it at the Kodak museum in New York City and put a copy in the window of his studio. Graça, who had given up trying to speak English by her ninetieth birthday, called him *o homen dos retratos*, the man of the photographs. He called her Grandma Balshor.

"She touched many lives. She had that magic about her." Marie said.

For Graça's ninety-second birthday, the family held a surprise party at a local restaurant. As always, Graça had a poem to recite. "Grandma never learned to read or write, but she could recite poetry by the hour." They poured her some Lancer's wine. Marie laughed. "Grandma Balshor gulped everything she ever drank. They poured about this much, and she took that thing and down the hatch. And so she put her glass down and said, 'Boys, carry me gently to my grave. First pour in the wine and cover me with whiskey.' It's beautiful in Portuguese when you say it, but I always remember that part." Two weeks later, Graça died.

Marie has filled her house with gifts, photographs, and memories. She and Al have become honorary grandparents to all the kids in the neighborhood, playing Santa Claus at Christmas, hosting annual Easter egg hunts in their yard, and raising funds for multiple sclerosis research and other causes.

On one wall of their dining room, portraits of Maria and Graça hang over written histories of the Sequeira and Balshor families. Marie has placed a tiny angel atop each photo. The two women are her angels looking down on her, watching her every minute of every day, she said.

THE PORTUGUESE WOMAN of the 1990s knows that her foremothers let men rule them like kings, and she says *basta*, enough!

Both in the United States and in Portugal, Portuguese women are claiming greater independence after centuries of submission to men. Traditionally, girls grew up sheltered and directed by their father's wishes. When they married, the wife moved wherever the husband wanted to go, served him like a master, and gave up her career dreams to take care of husband and family.

Until the 1970s, women in Portugal were legally on par with children. They could not travel abroad without their husbands' permission, nor could they carry on an occupation or profession, contract debts, or buy or sell property. They could not hold important political offices. Even their possessions, including the dowry they brought into the marriage, were owned by their husbands. The husband was the official head of the household unless he was incapacitated, absent, or dead. In short, women had no rights.

The old-fashioned Portuguese laws held women back for years. While American women had been voting for almost fifty years,

Portuguese women did not win full political equality until the 1976 constitution was adopted. They have made great progress since then. Today women hold numerous government posts. Maria de Lourdes Pintasilgo became Portugal's first female prime minister in 1979. However, women in government are still far outnumbered by men.

No matter what was happening in Lisbon, in Portuguese homes, females were restricted not only by sexist laws but by longstanding social customs. Young women lived with their parents until they married. Many went to school for only a few years before dropping out to help at home. If they went away to school, they lived in a convent or with relatives. On dates, a chaperone had to go along, even after the couple was engaged.

Once they were married, most Portuguese women stayed home with their children. It was socially acceptable for the men to have extramarital affairs, but not for the women. During social gatherings, the wives sat quietly while their husbands spoke. Some older Portuguese women remember men and women eating in separate rooms at family gatherings. The women would serve the men first, then retire to the kitchen for their own meals.

Most husbands did not want their wives to have jobs outside the home. In a 1975 survey quoted by Francis Rogers in *Atlantic Islanders*, only 25 percent of married women in Portugal were employed, compared to 49 percent in the United States.

As a teenager, Pauline Correia Stonehill found out that boys and girls did not have the same rights. When she was a child, the California dairy where she grew up was her playground, but as puberty approached, her father literally drew a line in the dirt and ordered her not to cross it. He no longer let her play anywhere near the male workers at the dairy for fear they would take advantage of her. Meanwhile, her brother was virtually running the ranch from the time he was twelve years old because their father was often away, working to organize dairymen throughout the state. Pauline resigned herself to helping her mother at home, but she didn't like it. "I felt like I was being discriminated against."

Her father was treated like a king in their house, Pauline added. The children were taught to defer to him in every way. They were never supposed to make noise, cry in front of him, or question what he said. If they wanted something, they were to ask once, accept the answer they were given, then go away when they were excused.

Men were even more dominant in the old country. Marie Balshor was shocked at the sexism she saw on her first trip to Portugal. When she was looking for her cousin, she saw a woman coming toward her with a jug on her head. "She looked so old. She probably was my age (early forties). Oh, but they age. In Portugal, the men will be in the *taberna* (tavern), and the women will be out there slaving. It's awful. I saw that with my own eyes.

"When I went to the village, somehow we hit the right house or somebody directed us, and there is my cousin's husband with a tie on in his house, and his son's in the house, and I said, 'Where's Maria?' 'Oh, you know today's the day that we all get water, and Maria and her mother are with the water out in the field.' Right then and there, I thought, oh baby. And lo and behold, here she comes; word got out that I was there. I loved her from the moment I met her. But the husband was the one that did all the talking about things."

Coming to America changed the family dynamics for many Portuguese women. Often the wife had to leave the shelter of her home to take a job in order to help the family survive. That introduced her to other people and other ways. She spent time away from the family and earned her own money for the first time in her life.

For many Portuguese couples, immigration started with a period of separation. The husband or sweetheart left first to find a job and save enough money to send for his mate. Meanwhile, she was on her own. That gave her a taste of independence, and she was loathe to give it up when they got back together.

Working outside the home made it harder for women to do everything inside the home. Back in the old country, working women often had servants. Those who couldn't afford servants could call on family members to help with childcare, cooking, and other chores.

Coming to America, where women, although still restricted by sexism, had the same legal rights as men, everything was suddenly different. Their more liberated American neighbors urged them to speak up for themselves and demand respect from their husbands.

Meanwhile, in Portugal, women grew restless as the nation moved from a dictatorship into a republic. They wanted the same freedoms their husbands enjoyed. Revolution did come for Portuguese women, albeit more slowly than it did for women in the United States. The book *Three Marias*, published in 1972, was a big influence. Written in the form of letters between three friends named Maria, it revealed the suffering of Portuguese women left at home by husbands fighting wars abroad or working on a distant continent.

In 1977, an anonymous Azorean woman published an even more radical book, *Loves of the Bitch Named "Pure,"* which exposed the repression of women that had been kept secret for so long. But things are looking up, she wrote. "The new Portugal of the Revolution is changing rapidly on the sexual front. Young women are even chasing the bulls on Terceira. When that happens, men and boys no longer have any reason to strut, to lord it over the other sex."

Today, Portuguese women have more rights, although they lag behind men in leadership roles—as they do in America. Although many women, both in Portugal and the United States, still make their main career finding and catering to a good husband, others are getting an education and going into business, engineering, and other fields. Especially in America, where their non-Portuguese classmates and friends urge them to break out of the traditional roles, young women defy the old rules.

Louise Pitta Polsky's maternal grandmother came to the United States alone. Although she had only four years of education, she wanted all of her children to be college-educated. She was the letter writer in the family and spent hours reading. "She would rather read than keep house," Louise said. Louise admits that her grandmother wasn't much of a housekeeper, and the one time she tried to sew a hem it came out "moon shaped," but she is proud of her grandmother for living life her own way.

Mary Ann Cabral also shunned traditional feminine ways. "I was actually a big old tomboy," she said. "Being on the ranch, I loved being outside. My mother used to get mad at me because I never wanted to do anything in the house. And I was always outside working with my dad, chasing the horses, feeding the cows, or out on the farm. I was doing a man's job, and I enjoyed it. We'd get up early in the morning, and when I went to bed at night I was tired.

"I still don't know how to sew. I can cook, clean, and that stuff, but I can't sew a straight line. I can't even crochet. Not me. I was a farm girl. The rougher the job, the better for me. To this day, I still love the outdoors."

Most women spent their lives at home, doing laundry, taking care of kids, or cooking for the men who worked on the ranch, Mary Ann said. When she was a kid, they all helped harvest corn. Her mom and aunt cooked for the men. The kids rode horses and rigged wagons. "Women were washing and ironing and staying home, but I wasn't going to do that."

Her sister-in-law Lucille Cabral had a different view. Girls today have too much freedom and are taking on too much, with both outside jobs and home cares, she said. "They've got their job concerns and their family concerns. I'm not saying they're bad to the kids, but it seems like it's different than we were. I'm not sorry that we stayed home. I was a housewife. That's what I thought we were supposed to be."

Mary Ann and Lucille taught both their sons and daughters to help around the house. With the wives working, the men have to share the load. "That's what I tell them," Lucille said. "When she works, you help her, but if she's not..." Some of her neighbors used to warn her that she was turning her sons into sissies, but they learned skills they're using now, she added.

"It's got to be fifty-fifty," Mary Ann said.

As much as laws may change, old customs hang on. Men still rule most Portuguese American homes, especially those of recent immigrants. A woman who is still working in San Jose's Portuguese community put it bluntly, "Portuguese men have this proudness about them. They're like roosters."

Portuguese women are passive and shy, said Nazaria Soares, who was born in the Azores. Everything is for the husband and children. The wives stay home and cook and crochet. They live for their children, but the children don't live for them. They kill themselves working for the family. They submit totally to the husband and do almost nothing for themselves.

Even if they have jobs, the women bear responsibility for all the household work. Portuguese men are always worrying about their manhood, Nazaria said. They have to prove their machismo, that they are not homosexuals. They can't do woman's work *"porque não são coisas de homens"* (it isn't manly). One of the things that attracted her to her Mexican American husband was that he was not afraid to hold her purse for her, she added.

Both men and women may oppose men doing domestic chores in traditional families. "It is not nice for a man to do woman's work. It is embarrassing," wrote Caroline Brettell, quoting the typical Portuguese attitude. "Women, as well as men, will taunt a man for doing housework with the epithet *marica* (sissy)," she added.

In Portugal, women have dreams of powerful careers, but most never see them come true, especially if they marry. The Portuguese and Latin cultures are very negative, Nazaria said.

She came to the United States when she was fifteen and found herself more fettered by her parents than the other kids were. "You don't get out of the house until you're married. Old-fashioned." When she was in college, she declared her independence. "I said, 'I put up with it before I was twenty-one. Now I don't.'" Nazaria's dream was to be a teacher, and she has made that dream come true. She teaches English and Portuguese.

Manuela Torres considered herself a career woman when she met her husband through a church group in Toronto. They dated,

Nazaria Soares and her son, Justin, 1997

then broke up for a while, partly because of her liberated attitude. "No man would tell me what to do," she said. Gualter was used to old-fashioned Portuguese women, not strong-minded females like Manuela. "That was okay as a friend, but it was not okay as a girlfriend. 'She's gonna boss me around, she's not gonna let me be like the Portuguese male.'"

Still, their common interests kept Manuela and Gualter together, and they married after a brief courtship. It wasn't always easy. Manuela continued working after their son was born and found a conflict between work and home life. "My husband understood about my career, but he couldn't figure out that I would put the career above him and my son. He was getting annoyed, to say the least." At that point, she was playing a key role at work and felt heavy responsibilities there as well as at home. Looking back, she said, she might have done things differently. After all, important as she thought she was, the bank didn't go out of business when she left.

Part of the move toward independence for Portuguese American women comes from society. Divorce, lack of money, and other factors are forcing Portuguese women who never considered careers to venture out of their homes. For many, it's a frightening move.

"I look around, and I see so many women that don't know what's happening. They don't know what hit them," Goretti Silveira said. "Somehow, all the things they were told were going to happen— they're not happening. They're not ready to be an individual."

Goretti herself has always been independent and had a career. She was also involved with her husband in many Portuguese activities. After fifteen years, her marriage ended in divorce, leaving her to plan life on her own.

In her family, Goretti said, her father was typically macho but not as bad as some. "Was he sexist? Yes. Was there a possibility of a 'no' on this question? I think not. But Mom had all the freedom in the world. He was never a jealous person. He might tell me my dress was too short, and he'd tell Mom her dress was too long."

Instead of holding her mother back, Goretti said, "On the contrary. He got to depend a lot on her." Certainly he believed women should and shouldn't do certain things, but his job back in the Azores took him to Lisbon twice a month, and things were changing there. Goretti was the first girl in her town to wear slacks when she wasn't going to a picnic. Her father brought her the pants from Lisbon.

Goretti, who kept her maiden name when she married, said her grandmother was the first feminist she knew. "She definitely depended on my grandfather for everything, but psychologically she was very independent. She ran the household and she also told me, 'Don't depend on men. You can't depend on men.'"

The older women back in the Azores were stuck in their traditional roles, Goretti said. "There were no options. I don't think we can begin to understand. I look at myself and all the options I have, and how I continue setting limitations."

Portuguese American women typically take the lead role in household chores. Their husbands may help, but the women are still mainly responsible, Goretti noted. "We think we have come a long ways. Women are going crazy, too, trying to keep the house and do the cooking and the baking, just like our mothers, and at the same time trying to have a career—and we're trying to do it better."

In that respect, things were easier in Portugal, Goretti said. "The few career women that I was raised with back in Portugal, they weren't expected to do anything but their jobs. There's a difference here." She knew a teacher in Portugal who had three servants and a seamstress, and that was not unusual.

Although the man has officially been the boss in Portuguese homes for centuries, many will privately admit that within the confines of their home, the woman holds the real power. "Ma was the boss," said Richard Alves of his mother, Mary. His wife, Kay, added, "Pa had the patience of a saint. He loved her enough that whatever Mary wanted was fine."

Soft-spoken Delia Mendes was straightforward when asked if her husband Ludovico rules the house. "Oh no, I'm in charge," she laughed. "Really, it's kind of equal."

Marie Gambrel credits her mother with teaching her how to handle the family finances. "I knew how to take care of business because I used to watch my mother. She used to take care of things."

Sylvia Carroll's grandmother knew how to get what she wanted. When she and her husband first married, they had no electricity or running water in the house. Grandma Rose wanted indoor plumbing, but Grandpa José resisted. She simply waited until he was away from home and had the bathroom put in. "She was an independent woman and very spunky," Sylvia recalled proudly. Her grandmother was tiny, barely five feet tall, and she limped most her life from a bad hip, but she was powerful in her quiet way.

Pat Silva Corbera believes she and her sister inherited their bossiness from her mother. Her father was a laid-back man who let his wife manage the household. "My mother was just a take-charge woman," she said. In Pat's own generation, "We rule the roost."

Deolinda Avila, like many Portuguese American women of her generation, is always on the go. With her job, her classes, volunteering for the Portuguese lodge, and taking care of her elderly parents, her grown daughters, and her husband, she feels as if she never has enough time. It has been a long time since she was a full-time housewife. "Sometimes I wonder what it was like."

"The Portuguese women are very strong," Maria Sykora said. "I think the Azorean women are more so because, if you look at history, the men went away a lot, either to sea or out to work." The women ran the households and cared for the children while their men were in the United States, Canada, South America, or on the ocean somewhere on a whaling boat. They learned to take care of themselves, Maria added.

Slowly, the new ways infiltrate into Portuguese American women's lives as they combine their new-found freedom with the strength they have always possessed. Their Americanized daughters claim the same rights their brothers have. For them, the man has never been the boss.

5

You Want to Go to School? What For?

 GORETTI SILVEIRA concluded a conversation in Portuguese with one of her staff at Jardim Infantil Dom Dinis, greeted me with a Portuguese kiss on both cheeks, and urged me to follow her on tiptoe through the rows of preschoolers sleeping on blankets on the floor in the next room. When we reached her office, she closed the door, waved me to a chair, and collapsed with a sigh. "Now we can talk."

It was a late afternoon in June 1992. She had already worked a full day teaching at San Jose High Academy around the corner. As owner of Jardim Infantil Dom Dinis, the only Portuguese preschool in the area, her days were long and full.

"I come here to play," Goretti grinned. After serious classes in Portuguese language and culture, English, and social science, she gets down on the floor with the children to play house, fingerpaint, and build things with blocks. She has no children of her own, but is close to all of her students—the big ones and the little ones.

The preschool was an oasis of child-sized chairs and tables, miniature kitchens for playing house, and cubbyholes for children's toys and sweaters. Children's artwork and photographs of toddlers in graduation gowns covered the walls.

Jardim Infantil Dom Dinis, named after the Portuguese king known as "The Educator," averaged thirty to fifty students, most of them Portuguese or Latin American. Parents came from all over the valley to bring their students there. I could hear Portuguese being spoken softly in the next room. Visitors were greeted with "*Boa tarde. Como vai?*" Eighty percent of the students were at least half Portuguese.

Goretti knew what it was like to be an immigrant struggling in the American school system. She was fourteen when her family left the Azores in 1966. Public school in São Jorge only went up to fourth grade, but her parents sent her to a private convent school. That education helped her survive when she arrived in California. Goretti was fluent in Portuguese and French but not in English.

"I spent those three years in high school learning English. Basically that's all I learned. It was good that my background was strong. Nobody can afford to lose three years of education, but at least I could afford it better than some other people."

She almost didn't get to come to America. Her father wanted her to stay in the convent school, where she was getting a good education. But her teacher convinced him that a year in America would help her learn English. Knowing how many Portuguese teens dropped out to help support the family, the teacher insisted, "If you take her, it's to go to school, not to go to work."

After graduating from Gunn High School in Palo Alto, Goretti went on to junior college, then Santa Clara University, earning a bachelor's degree in Spanish and French. From there, she attended the Monterey Institute of International Studies. Her career plans were uncertain, but when she was offered a teaching job, she accepted it. Growing up in São Jorge, she had always wanted to be a teacher. "The only woman that had a job at that time was my teacher, so she was my only role model."

Her foreign language education and teaching experience led to her job at San Jose High Academy in 1978. She worked with students there who needed to learn English or, knowing English, wanted to learn about the Portuguese language and culture. "I'm amazed, to tell you the truth, to see so much interest," Goretti said. "They are really thirsty for some roots, I think."

At a time of day when most high school teachers might be going home to relax, Goretti hurried to the preschool, where a loyal staff had kept things going the rest of the day. There she

Goretti Silveira and three students from Five Wounds School, 1997

continued her labor of love: helping children and parents caught between the American and Portuguese cultures.

Tiptoeing back through the rows of sleeping children, Goretti looked at her tiny students fondly. They were getting a head start on education, and maybe some of them would grow up to be teachers like her.

Five years later, some of those preschoolers had gone on to Five Wounds Elementary School and so had Goretti. She left San Jose High in 1993 to become principal at Five Wounds, where a large percentage of the students are Portuguese. She moved her preschool to the former convent on campus and continued to work there as well.

On a warm spring afternoon, Five Wounds School was quiet. A statue of the Virgin Mary watched over the lobby. Photos of the founding priest, the archbishop, and the pope were flanked by Easter bunnies and photos of each graduating class. The Portuguese nuns who used to run Five Wounds School were gone, replaced by lay teachers. Everyone spoke English here now, except the children who came once a week for special after-school classes in Portuguese.

Goretti had been principal for four years and was looking forward to retiring in June. She had intended to do that four years earlier, but Father Leonel Noia, pastor of Five Wounds Church and a personal friend, asked her to apply for the principal job. "I was going to plant an herb garden. I was going to read and write," she said with a sigh. Instead, she became a school principal. Suddenly, she had four times the responsibility she had before. She was overseeing preschool through eighth grade, a total of 325 children. During the school year, she had no time off, even on weekends. "It was a crash course in school administration," she said.

The time since the first interview had also been challenging in other ways. Goretti and her husband of fifteen years divorced. Although they remained partners in the preschool, they planned for Goretti to take over sole ownership. Goretti also joined two friends to start a publishing business, Bridge Publications. Its first two books were both about the Portuguese.

When we talked, Goretti was counting the days until she finished her term as school principal in June. She would continue to run the preschool, but with only one job instead of two, she hoped to finally plant those herbs and have time to read. She might go home to São Jorge for a while. But at forty-five, with an overabundance of energy, it seemed unlikely Goretti Silveira would retire for long, not with a new group of children ready for school every September.

MOST AMERICAN YOUTHS take their education for granted, at least through high school. For those with good grades, college is a given. After all, how can you get a good job without a degree? But for the early Portuguese immigrants and their children, education was a luxury they couldn't always afford.

It was common for pre-1920s immigrants to be illiterate. Back in Portugal, education was not required past fourth grade, and many children didn't even go to school that long. Until 1950, girls did not have to attend school at all. Schools were scarce in the rural areas, and the youth were needed at home to help take care of their large families and work on the family farm or dairy. For women especially, school seemed superfluous. Why spend years learning about literature, mathematics, and the outside world when they were destined to marry a man from their village and stay home with their children, just as their mother and grandmother had done?

Even in recent years, only the wealthy had access to good schools. Maria Sykora, who attended a Catholic girls school until her family left São Miguel when she was ten, said those with money can get a good education in Portugal. Those who can't afford to send their kids to private schools do without, although the situation has improved in the last few decades. Her own mother never went to school and is still unable to read or write.

Graça Balshor had no education. She worked in the fields from the time she was old enough to walk. "She never sat at a school desk," said Marie Balshor, her daughter-in-law. When she needed to sign something, Graça made an X. When Graça was sixty-five and applying for social security, Marie decided to teach her how to sign her name. She worked with her for about an hour, guiding Graça's hand, helping her write "Grace Balshor." Then she let her try it herself.

"She threw the paper and the pencil up in the air and said, 'For sixty-five years I haven't needed it, and I don't need it now.' But nobody could fool her on money, and she had a marvelous memory."

Typical of the earliest immigrants, my great-grandmother, Anna Souza, never learned to read or write in Portuguese or English. When her children needed affidavits in lieu of birth certificates (destroyed in a fire at the Santa Clara Mission) so they could sign up for social security, Grandma Souza signed with an X and had people witness her signature.

"When they came here, they went out and they worked," said Edna Sousa, Anna's daughter-in-law. Anna already had one child when she and her husband, Manuel, arrived in the United States, and then they had six more. They lived in a neighborhood of Portuguese immigrants and didn't need English to get along. After her husband died, Anna worked at a local cannery to support her family.

Edna told of a friend named Mary. "All she did was work on her father's dairy. The idea was to help the mother with the cooking and the cleaning and work out in the yard. She was so smart, but they didn't believe in education." Most women finished grammar school, then went to work or got married, and that was it.

Nellie McKee, Anna Souza's youngest daughter, quit high school six months shy of graduation. People told her she was a fool, but she responded, "Everything I want to know, I know." Much more interesting to Nellie was the job friends offered her at O'Brien's dry goods store, where she worked for thirteen years. Of the seven children in Nellie's family, only one brother graduated from high school. The rest quit to go to work.

Even those immigrants' children who went to school had a hard time. Language and cultural differences have long left Portuguese students wondering where they fit in. The Portuguese educational system is divided differently, and a student may already have studied history, math, and science, as well as one or more foreign languages, but it is difficult to even discuss what they already know when they don't speak English and therefore appear to know nothing.

Such was the experience of Amy Moody, who went to a one-room school on the island of Pico. She remembered writing on slates in lessons reminiscent of America's pioneer days. The teacher was her great aunt, a cruel woman who would hit her on the hand or pull her earlobe if she did a lesson incorrectly.

When she arrived in California, she was placed in a classroom in a small school in Turlock. She knew no English, but the other kids helped her, and the teacher taught her basic English after school.

"It's just learn as you go," she said. "I think of always being afraid to open my mouth because I was so afraid to say a word wrong."

Mary Ann Cabral, who was born here, remembered, "I didn't even know how to speak English when I went to kindergarten. I can remember trying to tell the teacher one day that I wanted to go to the bathroom. She couldn't understand what I was telling her. I had to go to the bathroom real bad. I said if you don't let me go, I'm going to wet the floor. I had to ask another kid if he knew how to say it. I was so embarrassed, and, oh, I couldn't say what I wanted to say. I was smart, but I stayed in kindergarten for two years because I couldn't speak English."

Mary Ann's education ended early. When she was in eighth grade, her mother became paralyzed. Mary Ann had to stay home to care for her and do some of the farm chores. A teacher came out to tutor her, and she went back to school for a while after her mother died, but she quit before she finished high school. "I never got anywhere in education, but I think I've done well for myself anyway."

Her sister-in-law Lucille Cabral didn't finish school either. Lucille's father was hurt while pruning trees and couldn't work. Then her mother was injured. As the oldest daughter, she spent so much time caring for her parents that she missed school half the time and finally quit after seventh grade. "I was spending more time at home than I was at school. I lost interest." Her parents didn't want her to quit, she said, but because she had to skip school whenever she was needed at home, she wasn't learning anything anyway.

Although many families shunned education as a waste of time, there were exceptions. Virginia Silveira said her mother's father and uncle insisted their children learn and hired a tutor to teach the family's ten children. "It was rather remarkable that they were studying Shakespeare. My mother was reading translations of *Romeo and Juliet* and *A Midsummer Night's Dream*."

Virginia's father's parents were very poor, but they also believed in education and taught themselves to read. "Each generation improves itself," Virginia continued. "Unfortunately, the Portuguese did not believe in educating women. My dad was a maverick in that department. His friends told him he was crazy to send me to college. We had friends who were very bright girls, and they didn't even send them to high school."

Virginia didn't realize that some people didn't know how to read until a cousin she was visiting in San Diego asked her to read a letter for her. She was shocked to discover a member of her own family was illiterate. "It really got to me. I thought, how could you go through life without reading. It's incredible."

Pauline Correia Stonehill was another exception. Her parents encouraged her to study. Her dairyman father was active in union and co-op affairs and spent a lot of time in town, which meant he could give her rides to and from extracurricular activities. Pauline went to the library often, took violin lessons, played in the school orchestra, acted in school plays, and also edited the school paper. "She did everything but sweep the floor," said her husband, Len.

Pauline was valedictorian for both her eighth grade and high school graduations. Her father supported her plans to go to college. As word got around, several of his male friends made special trips to the ranch to tell him he was wasting his money by sending a daughter to college. "He was a very unusual person," Pauline said. She was glad her father lived to see her working as a teacher.

Sylvia Carroll's Aunt Rose Peters, one of twelve children, was told that girls didn't need to go to high school. "She wanted desperately to go to school because she loved school, and she was very smart." Sylvia's grandmother disagreed with her husband and eventually prevailed. Aunt Rose finished high school and college. She worked for a newspaper in the 1930s and 1940s and was a teacher in the 1950s.

Sylvia's mother, Evelyn, was the youngest in her family. With her older sister paving the way, Evelyn went to the University of California at Berkeley. Both of the women did housework to pay their way, and both became teachers. Following in her mother's footsteps, Sylvia also worked as a teacher, although she later traded that career to work at a youth hostel in the Saratoga foothills.

Pauline Correia Stonehill playing her father's violin on her Confirmation day, 1935

Louise Pitta Polsky's grandmother was a "peasant woman who longed to be educated." She had only four years of formal education in Madeira before her mother died, and her father decreed that she would stay home and care for the family. Years later in California, she urged her children to go to college. All made it through high school, but only one son graduated from college. All of her grandchildren, however, have college educations. Although not a musician herself, Louise's grandmother also insisted that her children all have music lessons. "I don't know anyone else in that group who had piano lessons," Louise said.

Feeling too timid for UC Berkeley, especially after the family decided the university had turned her uncle into a communist, Louise went to Dominican College, a private Catholic college in San Rafael. "It exposed me to a lot of things that I hadn't been exposed to. Dominican kind of opened up the world to me." Louise majored in math, earned a teaching credential, and went on to a career as a middle school math teacher.

For Delia Mendes, a college education was out of the question, although she came to America in the 1960s, more recently than many of the immigrants who settled here. From age thirteen to seventeen, she cared for her widowed mother, who had cancer. She was lucky to graduate from high school in her native Pico. "You had to be rich to afford school," she said. "You work in the fields, get married, have kids. There's nothing else."

It's a different story in California. Delia's daughters laughed when asked if their mother wanted them to go to college. "Yes!" shouted Yvonne, the oldest, who is majoring in business administration.

Delia nodded. "I said, 'School first. Don't worry about working.'" All three of her daughters, eager for spending money, do have jobs, but they are also going to college. Delia said she went to college herself for a couple of years, but found it hard to balance her job, kids, and homework at the same time.

Dolores Freitas Spurgeon, whose grandparents emigrated from Madeira, received a twenty-five dollar PTA scholarship, enough to pay most of her first year's college fees, but her parents offered no help or support. "My father thought it was a waste," she said. The old-timers believed girls would just get married anyway. "As a result, I was determined to show him that it was not going to be a waste." She enrolled at San Jose State University, taking two majors—commerce and education—so she would be sure to get a good job.

Dolores went without most of her textbooks the first year because she couldn't afford them. She read at the library or borrowed her friends' books and somehow managed to earn C's or better in all her classes. Later, she worked in the campus offices to help pay for her schooling.

Despite these obstacles, Dolores graduated in 1936 with her elementary teaching credential and went to work at Jefferson Union School. When San Jose State started a journalism department, chairman Dwight Bentel hired her to work with him. At first, she did secretarial work, but she became an assistant instructor and, finally, a full professor. With Bentel's encouragement, she earned a master's degree and a general secondary credential at Stanford University.

Some families could only afford for one child to go to school. Edith Walter went to Heald College after high school. Her brothers, who stopped their educations after elementary school, paid her way. They later finished their high school studies in the U.S. military but were always embarrassed that they didn't graduate with others their age.

Even today, Portuguese youth, especially the girls, face obstacles in education. Goretti Silveira was lucky to have parents who supported her schooling; in fact, they insisted on it. "It was not an option for me. 'You're going to school, and that's all there is to it.'"

But as a teacher, she found it was not the same for many of her students. They might finish high school, but they didn't go on. "And we're talking about some really bright kids, especially the girls. They get married so soon." They didn't have the support at home, Goretti said. "The expectation is not there."

THE NEWEST IMMIGRANTS give education a high priority. Deolinda Avila started her education in Portugal. After her parents brought her to the United States, she attended local schools but fell behind. Her parents sent her back to the Azores to study while she lived with relatives. The only way her parents could afford to pay for her private education in the Azores was to live and work in the United States.

After graduation, Deolinda returned to California, but she has never stopped learning. She has taken classes at Foothill College, San Jose State University, and San Jose City College, dabbling in many different subjects, including sewing, psychology, English, history, and real estate. Every class has proved useful, she insisted. Now working as a teacher's aide in the Los Altos School District, she has been looking at class schedules again. "I want to take fun classes," she said. Another computer course or cake decorating or flower arranging are all possibilities. She earned her associate of arts degree at age forty-eight. At fifty, she was not sure she wanted to go for her bachelor's degree, but she was still interested in learning about anything she could. She confessed that she was waiting for a message from the Holy Spirit to tell her what would come next.

Mariel Fedrí came to California to go to college, earning her master's degree in foreign language at San Jose State. She became a Spanish instructor at Ohlone College in Fremont. Education is her joy and her crusade, she said. "Without education, you can't go anywhere."

Krista Harper, whose mother's family came from São Miguel, grew up in a family of educators. Her mother, father, and sister all have doctorates in education. Krista grew up discussing education and anthropology at the dinner table. It was natural for her to follow in her parents' footsteps and major in anthropology at the University of California at Berkeley. She finished her bachelor's degree at Berkeley with a senior honors project on pregnancy and childbirth among Portuguese women.

After graduation, Krista received a National Science Foundation scholarship to graduate school. Pursuing her Ph.D. in anthropology at the University of California at Santa Cruz, she spent her first summer doing research in São Miguel. She traveled from the Azores to eastern Europe and became fascinated with the Hungarian culture. Winning a Fulbright scholarship and an International Research and Exchanges Board grant, she spent two years in Hungary studying the environmental movement there. She came home in July 1997 and started working on her dissertation and looking for teaching jobs.

Although it was natural for Krista to go to college, it was a different story for her mother, Victoria De Motta Harper. A professor of elementary education and director of the Institute of Teaching and Learning at San Jose State University, Victoria was the first person in her family to go to college. Her mother, who worked as an electrician during World War II, had stopped school after eighth grade. Victoria married in her late teens but was determined to finish college, working as a secretary to pay her way.

Victoria's original goal was a degree in architecture, Krista said, but school officials steered her into early childhood education as a more appropriate field for a woman. Krista, growing up in a different era, had far more choices.

For some Portuguese women, it's never too late to pursue the education dream. Pauline Costa, daughter of Portuguese immigrants, grew up on a dairy farm in California's Central Valley. She left school at sixteen to get married. She had a child by the time she was eighteen and was working on a ranch with her husband. They had two more children and bought their own dairy farm.

At age forty-five and already a grandmother, Pauline went back to school to earn her high school diploma. Then she went on to junior college. Even when the dairy industry hit hard times and they lost their ranch, she took a job in town and kept going to school, driving fifty miles to Fresno State for night classes. She earned her degree in special education and began her teaching career at age fifty. In her sixties, she was named Tulare County Teacher of the Year; in her seventies, she continued teaching special needs students during the day and citizenship classes for Portuguese immigrants at night.

Many Portuguese American parents dream of a better education for their children than they had. It's part of the reason their ancestors left Portugal. In her book, *In the Absence of Men*, Caroline Brettell quotes a Portuguese man she met on a plane trip from Lisbon to New York. "My father," he said, "could neither read nor write, and yet he sent me to school. Now I want more for my children—a proper house and even more education. It is impossible to give them this with what I earn in Portugal, so I am on an adventure, going to America."

6

Grandma Never Learned English

"*SIM, FALO PORTUGUÊS*," I said, taking a deep breath. I had been studying the language with Nazaria Soares and felt just on the brink of being able to converse in Portuguese—if we didn't discuss anything too complicated. I had started learning Portuguese several years before, working with books and tapes in preparation for our first trip to the Azores. My high school Spanish studies both helped and confused me. The words were similar, yet different. I was still cramming at Los Angeles International Airport as we sat surrounded by our luggage, waiting for our flight to Terceira.

The flight attendant welcomed us in Portuguese. I responded, "*Gracias*," but I knew immediately it was wrong. That was Spanish. How did you say "thank you" in Portuguese? Embarrassed, I shut up and spoke English for the rest of the flight. Once I was in the Azores, surrounded by the Portuguese language, I could order simple meals and read road signs. Listening to speeches, going to mass, eavesdropping on conversations, I could comprehend only bits and pieces. But I wanted to understand, and I wanted to talk to the

Portuguese people all around us. I just didn't have the words. How many years would it take before I really grasped the language?

I had taken a course at Mission College and learned how to say things like "blackboard" and "notebook." But could I converse with the Azoreans in Little Portugal? No way. I attended meetings and *festas* feeling deaf and mute. Only when Nazaria forced me into one-on-one conversation about everyday topics did the language become real. I had to take that hard step of making mistakes, of trying to say things without knowing all the words.

"I don't know the verbs," I would complain, breaking into English.

"Don't worry about it, they will come," she assured me.

And they are beginning to. But I know firsthand how immigrants feel trying to survive in a language not their own.

Often, I can't find the precise words, so I say something that is not quite what I mean, and I don't always understand what the other person is saying. I get the general idea, but I misunderstand the details. I listen to Portuguese radio stations and read the Portuguese papers, then gratefully turn back to the English-language media. It just seems too hard to deal with Portuguese sometimes. When someone answers the telephone in Portuguese, my first instinct is to hang up rather than struggle to make myself understood. Immigrants to America must feel that way about English. It's no wonder they look for Portuguese stores, Portuguese doctors, and Portuguese priests.

My great-grandmother Anna Souza, who came from Faial in the late 1800s, never learned English. Insulated in a Portuguese section of Santa Clara, she could survive without it. Her children spoke both English and Portuguese and served as a buffer to the outside world. Her grandchildren spoke only English.

It's part of the Americanization process. Immigrants' children find themselves crippled by the lack of English when they go to school and are embarrassed to be seen as foreigners. Most children of immigrants learn English quickly. The young ones pick up the words from their older siblings, and soon everybody is speaking English except their parents.

In my grandparents' day, the children were pressed into service as interpreters. They became the family spokespersons at the market, the doctor's office, and the bank. When the children married, often to non-Portuguese spouses, they spoke English in their homes. The grandchildren knew only English, while Grandma was still speaking Portuguese. They lived in separate worlds. Many of the stories of the older generation have been lost because there was no common language with which to share them.

I have been learning Portuguese from strangers. My mother doesn't know the language well enough to teach me, but when I try out words she remembers from her childhood, she smiles. Suddenly we are bound by the language of our ancestors, like a secret code.

Grandma Souza never reached the point where she was comfortable speaking English beyond "yes," "no," and "thank you." How I wish she were still alive today so we could sit down together and really talk. "*Avó, agora falo português.*" Tell me about your life. "*Sim, falo português. Um pouco.*" Yes, I speak Portuguese. A little.

MANY OF THE PORTUGUESE WOMEN who emigrated to America in the early 1900s could not speak English. Not a word. Like their male counterparts, they landed by ship on the East Coast, climbed aboard a train with a destination tag attached to their coats, and rode across thousands of miles of unfamiliar territory, hoping somebody would tell them when to get off. Once they left the train in California, with luck greeted by friends or family members, they clung together, fearful of encountering anyone who wasn't Portuguese.

It was not unusual for older Portuguese immigrants to remain hidden in their new communities their entire lives, sending their children, unfamiliar with the English language, off to American schools. The fathers might be forced to speak English when they went to work, but Mama stayed home.

That's the way it was with Mary Souza Cabral's mother. Her husband learned English to conduct his business, and the kids picked it up at school. "It doesn't take long for kids to learn," Mary said with a smile. But her mother got by with gestures and a few broken words.

Pauline Correia Stonehill's dad spoke very little English when he got married. The family spoke Portuguese at home until the kids went to school. Pauline started out speaking Portuguese, but gradually switched to English. Her middle brother spoke a little of both languages. Her youngest brother never spoke Portuguese at all. "Eventually we were all speaking English," she said. Her last words to her father were in English, she added.

Lucille Cabral's mother never learned English. "She could write her name, that was it." She couldn't read or write Portuguese either. "She didn't have hardly any education, from what I understand. She had such a large family. She had to go out in the fields and work. She was one of the oldest ones. I think she's the only who didn't know how to write. My other uncles and aunts all did."

As they became Americanized, many children were embarrassed by their mothers, who spoke only Portuguese and were obviously foreign. When their friends were nearby, they often pleaded, "Hush, Mama. Don't talk so loud."

Once they learned English, the children served as interpreters for their parents. "Every time they went to the grocery store, they had to take their little kids with them to speak for them," Bea Costa said.

However, the parents often knew more English than they let on. They were able to conduct bilingual conversations with their grandchildren and deal with the outside world when they had to. When Lorraine Freitas took her mother out to eat after a doctor's appointment, Lorraine asked in Portuguese, "Mama, how do you know how to order? You don't speak English."

Her mother responded, "Never mind. I know how to say 'a piece of pie and a cup of coffee.'"

Nellie McKee laughed, recalling her mother's knowledge of English. "Don't worry. If you came to the door and tried to sell her something, she'd understand. She'd get rid of them in a hurry. She could say yes and no and shake hands and stuff like that, but she used mostly Portuguese."

Mary Giglitto's family was an exception. Her mother learned English and her children learned Portuguese so they could communicate with each other. Her daughter also learned Italian, the language of her father's family. However, Mary said, her nieces and nephews don't speak any Portuguese.

The urge to seem American was strong among the Portuguese Americans. Amy Moody's father went to night school to learn English and insisted the entire family learn. "For a while, we sort of lost the Portuguese culture because we wanted to be Americans."

When Sylvia Carroll's grandfather married his second wife, Rose, she acquired a ready-made family. Handicapped by knowing only Portuguese when she went to school, Rose told her new husband her children were going to speak English. From then on, he spoke to them in Portuguese, and they replied in English.

One of these children, Evelyn, was Sylvia's mother. "She never spoke Portuguese in any way at all," Sylvia said. The only words she passed down to her kids were a couple of expressions, *pobrezinha* (poor little thing) and *credo* (an expression of disgust).

Like Sylvia, I learned only a few words pertinent to young children. *Casinha* was the bathroom, and *palmada* (a little slap) was what I would get if I didn't behave. A *babão* (nitwit) was somebody too stupid for his own good.

Virginia Silveira learned English from her English-speaking neighbors and school companions. "I went to school when I was four, and from that day on, I did not speak one word of Portuguese. I heard it, I understood it, but by God you'd have had to pillory me to make me speak it."

STRUGGLING TO KEEP UP with their English-speaking peers at school, Portuguese American youth needed to learn English as quickly as possible. Because she didn't know English when she arrived from Pico, Amy Moody's sister started grammar school at age sixteen.

After a year, she progressed into high school. She later went on to college and became a teacher, her lifelong ambition.

Marie Gambrel was born in the United States, but knew only Portuguese when she started school. As a result, she did poorly and her teacher kept sending notes—written in English—home to her mother. Her father refused to let his children practice English. "In this house, we don't speak anything else but Portuguese," her father ordered.

Once she learned enough English to get by, Marie started taking her little brother aside to teach him what she knew. "I said, he's not going to go through what I went through." If they heard their father coming in the door, they stopped, but by the time Marie's brother started school, he was ready.

Marie Balshor also began school without being able to communicate. Her older brother decided one day in March to take her to school. "I didn't even know my name. I only knew I was Maria. He just took me and left me in this class." She vividly remembers the other kids staring at her and making "go away" gestures. The teacher pinned a note on her blouse with the message that school starts in September, and she should come back then.

Once she did go to school, she did well in math, but struggled when it came to language. "I had 'promotion endangered' two times because I didn't know the language, and there was nobody to help me at home. But I had determination, and I learned."

Marie believes today's immigrant children have it too easy. "This bilingual program that they've got in the school systems now, I'm just so against it, because it builds character in people when you have to really study and do something for yourself. If I can do it, anybody can do it. Too much money is going in that direction that doesn't need to. I feel that I became the person that I am today because of all the adversity that I had growing up."

THESE DAYS, many descendants of Portuguese immigrants bemoan the loss of their parents' language. They enroll in classes and ask their family for words. The sound is familiar, but the mechanics of Portuguese have been lost.

When Dolores Freitas Spurgeon visited Portugal, she regretted not knowing the language better. The words came slowly. "I couldn't always say what I was feeling."

Jane Rose, who operated a fitness salon in Santa Clara, asked her Portuguese customers to speak only Portuguese. Although she grew up listening to her grandmother speak the language, her Portuguese faded away as she worked to perfect her English.

Edith Walter remembers that the only time her family openly spoke Portuguese in public was at the annual *festas*. She used to speak the language with her mother and mother-in-law, but now that both are gone, she has no one to talk to. Sometimes she tries to think in Portuguese just to keep up the language, she said.

Sylvia Carroll, who didn't learn Portuguese from her Portuguese mother, majored in Spanish in college and took a course in Portuguese at UC Berkeley, but she didn't get very far with it, especially since she had no one to practice with. Her Portuguese improved when she arrived in Little Portugal and rented an apartment across from Five Wounds Church. The neighbor she hired as a babysitter for her daughter was an immigrant from Faial and spoke very little English, so Sylvia was forced to communicate in her broken Portuguese. A few years later, when she started teaching English classes to immigrants, some of her students were Portuguese, so the language came in handy.

When Pat Silva Corbera conversed with her father, "It would be four words in Portuguese and two in English." Her mother spoke English, but her dad never quite mastered the language. Pat was amazed that he could read and understand an American newspaper. Now she's the same way with Portuguese. She understands the language but can't carry on a conversation.

Josephine Silva went back to school at age thirty-seven to study Portuguese language and culture. Before she visited Portugal, she

Sylvia Carroll, 1997

studied hard and was able to make herself understood, she said. Her husband, who grew up speaking Portuguese, depended on her in the Azores.

Patricia Borba McDonald remembers with frustration that her family did not pass down the Portuguese language. Her mother could speak it but couldn't write it. Patricia doesn't know Portuguese at all. "I think there's a whole generation lost," she said.

As in many families, Cristina Mendonsa's grandparents used Portuguese when they didn't want the kids to know what they were talking about. Although she does not speak Portuguese, Cristina said, "I love listening to the language. I used to listen to my grandmother talk it. She would sing in Portuguese as she was preparing meals or whatever, just kind of hum or sing to herself in the kitchen, and it was very soothing. It's a very soothing language; I love to listen to it. I know only the things my father told me, like *come e calate*, shut up and eat, or *feche a porta*, shut the door—little things like that they would tell me to do."

Marie Gambrel, who struggled so hard to learn English, now regrets that she didn't teach her sons Portuguese. "The saddest thing that I didn't do is teach them Portuguese. I was home. I could have been talking to them all day in Portuguese." Once in a while, she will say a few Portuguese words to her sons, things like *dame um abraço* (give me a hug). "It just didn't dawn on me 'til later," she said, perhaps because her husband was not Portuguese. "When I talk about it, I just want to cry because they only know words, that's all."

PORTUGUESE IMMIGRANTS struggle with their American children, urging them to use the language. Amy Moody's children don't speak Portuguese. Neither does her husband, Steve, who is also of Portuguese descent, nor her sister and her husband. Although she believes in the melting pot concept, she wishes they had not lost their parents' language. Amy made an effort to speak only Portuguese when she went back to Pico with her parents for a visit. After a few days, the words came back to her. Her parents helped when she got stuck. "It's rude not to speak their language," she said, "especially if you're family."

When Deolinda Avila speaks to her kids in Portuguese, they groan, "Oh Mom, speak English."

"My girls understand Portuguese, but at home they never speak Portuguese unless they are forced to talk to the grandparents or other people that don't speak English," Deolinda said. "When they visit the relatives in the Azores, they speak Portuguese. Here, they prefer English."

Donna Gomes Austin's daughter Nicole learned Portuguese when she went to work in Brazil and fell in love with a Brazilian man. Her mother knows only bits and pieces of the language, but Nicole can converse with her grandmother Eva Gomes in Portuguese now. Donna was hoping her mother would join their family in Brazil to serve as interpreter at Nicole's wedding. "We won't have a clue what's going on unless you sit next to us and tell us," she told her. Eva claimed she didn't know much Portuguese, that she hadn't had anyone to speak it to since her husband died thirty years ago, but Donna countered, "Oh, she speaks it very well."

Donna loves to tell a story about her daughters and the Portuguese language. Shortly after her daughters started school, their teacher asked which students spoke a foreign language. Twins Nicole and Kristen raised their hands. The teacher then contacted Donna, worried that the school would have to test the girls and make special provisions to teach them English. No, no, Donna said, they only knew a few words of Portuguese.

"Another day in class, the teacher asked Nicole to give her a Portuguese word. Nicole, who knew only a few, said '*Mais fica*,' which means 'More for me.' The teacher said, 'Okay class,' and the whole class said, '*Mais fica*.' And then Mrs. Chung had to come in and tell me about the word, and my heart stopped because I didn't know what word she was going to be telling."

Mary Anne Cabral said she tried to teach her kids the language, but they always responded in English. Now they complain that she should have taught them. Since her father died, she struggles not to forget the words herself. She speaks in Portuguese to her cousins on the phone and asks them to fill in the words she has forgotten.

Those who have kept up the language use it to help more recent immigrants, translating in schools, hospitals, and other places. When her children were young, Bea Costa was often called to the school to help translate. Once she got a call about two new boys who showed up at school with no idea what to do. "Somebody told that Portuguese mother that if you put those two boys on the bus that those two boys are going to get to school. Now these kids couldn't speak English, right? They get to school, what are they going to do with them? 'Who are you? Where do you live?' They don't know." Bea picked up the boys and drove them around until they found their house, then explained to the mother that the children had to be registered, have all the required vaccinations, and then be placed in a class. She helped her do the paperwork to get her kids enrolled. Those boys are now grown and still come to see Bea at her store.

Deolinda Avila has often been called on to make phone calls and write papers for friends who don't feel comfortable communicating in English. She once accompanied a woman to the hospital at midnight to translate while she gave birth. For a while, she was very busy translating, until it got to be such a burden she had to cut back. People still ask her to translate or write letters for them. Sometimes she comes home and finds them at her door. "You use the gifts God gave you to help others," she said. "I never say, 'No, that's not my problem.'"

"It's come in handy, my Portuguese, really," said Lorraine Freitas. And sometimes in surprising places. On vacation in Southern California, she stopped at a department store where a yarn sale was going on. She heard a familiar language. A Portuguese woman and her husband had gone from floor to floor and couldn't find what they wanted. Lorraine stepped in and solved their problem. The store manager was so relieved he gave her her yarn for nothing. "Knowing Portuguese has been an asset, not a detriment in my experience. I have been in places where people are panicked—they can't communicate with the person." She turns around and asks, "Can I help you?"

Sometimes when driving, Lorraine thinks, "How could those people in those days get behind the wheel of a car and travel? They couldn't read the signs. They helped each other, that's what they did."

Nazaria Soares, a language teacher, speaks Portuguese, English, and Spanish. Her son, Justin, is also learning all three languages. Although Nazaria is an Azorean immigrant, her husband is Mexican. They try to speak only one of the three languages at a time and to speak correctly. Most of the private conversations between mother and son are in Portuguese. Nazaria knows that when Justin starts school, he will mostly speak English. Even for herself, it's confusing knowing more than one language, Nazaria said. "Sometimes I don't know whether I'm speaking English or Spanish."

Delia Mendes, whose family still speaks Portuguese at home, noted that her youngest daughter didn't know any English when she started kindergarten. The teacher didn't realize the problem until their first conference, when Delia explained that her children spoke only Portuguese. So that's why the girl didn't respond to what she was saying, the teacher said. Delia, who speaks English slowly with a musical accent, dropping most of her h's, learned English from television, her kids, and her job, she said.

At Five Wounds School, Principal Goretti Silveira said children come after school for Portuguese lessons. Some speak the language at home, while others know only a few words. The program is financed by the Portuguese government. Youths who pass the Portuguese equivalency tests become qualified to enter regular classes with their age group if their family decides to move back to Portugal, bringing the cycle of immigration full circle.

7

Portuguese Women Pray From the Heart

 WHEN EVA GOMES graduated from grammar school, going on to high school was out of the question. After the family moved from Hawaii to Santa Clara, California, they had fallen on hard times. Her father was unemployed, and the five kids had to do whatever they could to help. Eva took a job at a San Jose factory, sorting pickles. Her sixteen dollar weekly salary was enough to support the family for the year she worked there. Seventy-two years later, she can still remember the smell of pickles and brine.

Eva married Thomas Gomes when she was eighteen and spent the rest of her life in Santa Clara. They owned Gomes Market, a grocery store at Washington and Bellomy streets. The family lived in the apartments upstairs. In 1964, they moved to a house nearby, but they continued to run the market until Thomas's death three years later.

 EVA'S DAUGHTER DONNA made it through high school, but her father, who was running a successful business with only a third-grade education, was set against her going on to college. Donna knew she wanted more schooling, but hadn't taken any of the prerequisites to get into college. "I didn't really have a lot of guidance about education," she said.

Her solution? She came home from a Catholic retreat and announced that she was going to be a nun. "My mother came to pick me up, and I said, 'I'm entering the convent,' and she said, 'What?!!' And my father, oh, he just didn't believe I was going to, and of course the more he didn't believe it and ordered me to stay home, the more I wanted to go."

Becoming a nun enabled Donna to get the education she craved. Through the Notre Dame order, Donna earned her bachelor's degree at the College of Notre Dame, her master's degree at the United States International University in San Diego, and her teaching credential at San Jose State University. Although she left the order twelve years later, Donna still looks back on the sisters with gratitude. "I don't think I would have made it through college if I hadn't gone to the convent. In the convent, I got a real education, and I lived with some beautiful women."

Donna is honest but succinct about why she left the order. She became involved with an Irish priest in Chico, where she was working. He insisted that the Catholic church would soon allow priests to marry, but Donna didn't expect to see it in her lifetime. "I got on a Greyhound bus, and I just took off." She traded her habit for a borrowed skirt and blouse to wear on the trip, which seemed to last forever as the bus stopped at every town along the way. "That was the scariest thing I ever went through. I was terrified. It was like I was wearing my slip. I took off my veil last. Then I just got on the bus and came home." By that time, her father had died, but she remembers her brother was so angry about her leaving the convent that he wouldn't speak to her for quite a while.

Reminiscing at Donna's sprawling home in the Cupertino hills, Eva laughed at how her daughter spent hours watching the old "I Love Lucy" shows after she came home. While Donna had been in the convent, a lot had changed in the world, including the advent of color television and rock and roll. "Once I went into the convent, I never got to see anything. I missed all of those years from 1956 to 1968. I missed all the series, I didn't know the songs, I didn't know anything. They didn't let us read the newspaper, so I was catching up with all these things."

As a nun, Donna taught at parochial schools in Chico, Campbell, Saratoga, Santa Barbara, San Francisco, and Watsonville. When she returned to public life, she continued her career, teaching primary grades at Hester School in San Jose for twenty-five years. After a stint as a resource teacher at the San Jose Unified School District office, she happily returned to teaching first and second grades. Donna is a mentor teacher now. She has also served on the Cupertino planning commission and ran for city council in 1995.

Her years as a nun were a positive experience, Donna stressed, but she is satisfied with the results of her decision to leave. In those days, nuns were warned that if they left the order, they would never be happy, but Donna believes each person has to follow her own conscience. Although she stopped being a nun, she is still a practicing Catholic, as she has been all her life, since her mother helped her with her first catechism lessons.

Eva has always set an example of religious devotion for the family. At eighty-eight, she still gets up at 5:30 every morning to say her prayers and drives herself to the eight o'clock mass at St. Clare's church. "Oh yes, I love it," she said. "That's the highlight of my day. If I wouldn't do that, I don't know what I'd do."

Donna teased her mother about saying five rosaries a day.

"I guess that's why I'm still here," Eva replied.

A few years after leaving the convent, Donna married Scot Austin. Scot was a Baptist, but he agreed to raise their twin daughters in the Catholic faith. Nicole and Kristen attended a Catholic elementary school and continue to practice the faith as adults. Both twins married Catholic men in Catholic weddings.

Being married to a non-Catholic has not always been easy for Donna. "I got lukewarm for a while, after I got married." She struggled to get the whole family to attend mass with her every Sunday, but finally decided to just go for herself. She is an active member of St. Joseph's parish.

Catholicism is an integral part of the Portuguese culture, Donna said. In Portugal, every event is based on Catholic saints and feasts. Although she does not say five rosaries a day, she would never consider leaving the church, and she is proud her daughters have continued in the faith. "Being Catholic is not something you brag about or talk about. You just are."

In the small Azorean villages from which most Portuguese immigrants come, the church is the center of activity. Most of the feast days are based on religious holidays, the priest is the wise leader and educator, and everyday life is governed by the laws of the church. While there are some Portuguese Protestants and Jews, the Roman Catholic faith predominates.

In *Atlantic Islanders*, Francis Rogers writes, "The very calendar by which the islanders lead their lives is the church's, beginning with the names for the days of the week." The Portuguese calendar starts with the Lord's Day—Sunday (*domingo*)—and numbers the succeeding days. Monday is *segunda-feira*, Tuesday is *têrça-feira*, etc. The seventh day is the sabbath (*sábado*).

"Remembrance of Christian feasts and saints represents an intimate and meaningful experience for the insular Portuguese, who pray quite sincerely and honestly to a favorite saint and above all to the Virgin to intercede for them with God-the-Father or God-the-Son for divine intervention in connection with a physical affliction or even the loss of a simple object," Rogers continues. Children are christened with saint's names or versions of the name Mary. Even boats and airplanes are given saints' names and blessed by a priest.

The faithful flock to Fátima, north of Lisbon, to worship at the shrine where Mary is said to have appeared to three children. Portuguese women spend hours on their knees, moving slowly around the altar at Fátima. Stores surrounding the Fátima complex offer religious goods, from rosary beads to six-foot tall statues of Jesus and the Blessed Mother.

In Portuguese homes, crucifixes, "Sacred Heart" pictures of Jesus, and images of Mary abound. Tiles beside the front door depict religious images. Roadside grottos pay tribute to Mary, Jesus, or one of the saints. In Portugal, religion is very much a part of everyday life, and the immigrants brought their devotion with them to America.

When the early immigrants came to the United States, they were dismayed to find the Catholic churches different from those at home. Customs had changed, and the language barrier made it difficult to understand what the American priests were saying. As a result, many Portuguese communities built their own churches and imported priests from Portugal to lead their worship in their own language and the rituals they were used to.

One such church is Five Wounds—known in Portuguese as *Cinco Chagas*—built in San Jose in 1914. The imposing cathedral-like building, whose twin spires can be seen from Highway 101, is the center of the city's Portuguese district. Its priests, direct from the homeland, are included in every facet of community life.

Not all immigrants go to the Portuguese churches. The move to look, sound, and act American extends to religion for some. Edna Sousa said her father never liked Five Wounds Church. It was built with Portuguese money, and they were always asking for more, he said. So they went to St. Leo's in central San Jose. "We just went to church on Sunday and that was it," Edna said.

However, Edna and her sister Virginia did go to the *festas* at the Portuguese churches in Santa Clara and East San Jose. Edna marched in the parades. She was—and still is—active in the Young

Five Wounds Church, San Jose, 1997

Ladies Institute, a church service organization. The two sisters attend mass together every Sunday, not at a Portuguese church, but at one near their home.

Mary Cabral O'Reilly's family went to church regularly, first in the Central Valley, then in San Jose, where they attended Five Wounds and St. Clare's. Mary learned her prayers from her mother in Portuguese. Later, she taught her mother how to say them in English. They would sometimes say the rosary, alternating languages, one starting a prayer in English, the other finishing in Portuguese, or vice versa.

In Portuguese families, the women were often the religious leaders and men the reluctant followers. Pauline Correia Stonehill's father was typical of many. He would take them to the church door but wouldn't go in. He was so hostile to church authorities that he almost got himself excommunicated, Pauline said.

My mother was the religious mentor at our house, too. Each night we would go over our religious lessons and our prayers together. She took my brother and me to catechism and confession. When my uncle was paralyzed in a motorcycle accident, she led us in prayers to Mother Seton in hopes that she would effect a miraculous cure and earn her sainthood. We wore Mother Seton medals pinned to our undershirts every day. I remember standing in the restroom at school and praying hard. I could feel God there in that cold, tiled room.

Former state senator Henry Mello said his grandmother had the whole clan on their knees for nine days before every Christmas. She sang and they all prayed in Portuguese. To a boy, it seemed very long.

Germana Silvera Sarmento was deeply religious. When her daughter became paralyzed, Germana promised God that if her daughter walked again she would take herself to the Azores and help feed the poor. When her daughter recovered, Germana set out for the islands. She paid to have five steers butchered and many loaves of bread made, then threw a huge dinner for the people of the village.

The Portuguese people are very religious, Nellie McKee said. They go to church all the time, and they pray from the heart. She was always saying novenas—nine days of special prayers. People would call and ask her to pray for them, so she would add them to the list, doing novenas five times a day. Her tiny house—not far from St. Clare's Church—was filled with religious pictures and statues, and God's name was always on her lips.

Nellie's husband, Ollie, was not Catholic when they were courting. She told him that if he didn't convert, she wouldn't marry him, so he adopted her faith. He joined her at Sunday mass and worked with her at bazaars, card parties, and other church affairs.

Marie Gambrel's mother and grandmother were also religious. She can still picture her grandmother sitting in her rocker, praying with her rosary. She worried about everyone, especially about the folks driving the unpaved roads in the Pocket area where they lived. She passed her religious views to her daughter and granddaughters.

"Why did my sister become a nun? On account of my mother," said Marie, who is also a devout Catholic, although she doesn't drive and is unable to attend mass regularly.

In the old days, Catholics were required to fast before communion. After church they came home, changed their clothes, and shared a big Sunday meal. They had to feed the animals, but all other work was done before or after Sunday, Edith Walter said. "We'd go every Sunday. We'd sit in the second pew; that was our pew."

Until they moved to San Jose, they went to St. John the Baptist Church in Milpitas, going to confession on Saturdays and communion on Sundays. "If you didn't go to communion on Sunday, everybody would look at you." Her family said grace at every meal and prayed together every evening.

Delia Mendes's family would say the rosary around the table every night. She laughed, remembering that when they went to visit her grandparents, they would listen to see if they were still praying and wait outside until they finished.

Marie Balshor's mother, Maria Sequeira, one of fifteen children, was very religious. "I just don't know how she learned all this religion. I don't know how her mother and father even had the time to teach them." The family said the rosary nightly. Marie's mother would let her go to bed, but she couldn't sleep until the prayer was over. She would make her answer the prayers from her bed. "If I dozed off, it was 'Maria, Maria!'"

Her faith has been her lifeline since childhood, Marie says. "You really have to have a basis of life, and I think the basis of life is your religion. It has everything to do with what you really are. If you can follow the Golden Rule and the Ten Commandments, you've got it made. It's hard to follow the Ten Commandments, but if you can do that, even if times are tough, really that's all it takes. And simplify life. My mother lived all her life in those two little shacks put together. My mother never needed anything."

For Bea Costa, church is still a vital part of everyday life. "I'm the kind of person that I pray to God like I'm talking to somebody, like I'm talking to you. He's my friend." Bea used to pass the church on her way home from high school and would often stop by. "I'd walk in, say 'I had a rotten day, see if you can make it better tomorrow, goodbye.'" Her Jewish friend who walked with her would ask, "What kind of a way is that to pray?" "I'd say, 'He understands what I'm saying. If I talk to you like that, you understand. What makes you think that he doesn't understand?' And the next day, I'd say, 'I had a much better day. Thank you.'"

Her friend later became a Catholic. "It wasn't any talking on my part," Bea stressed. "She said, 'I want to have that kind of a relationship with my God.'"

Bea taught catechism for twenty-two years in Santa Clara. She knew all the children who were around her son's age. When she took over the class in the fourth grade, the teacher was having problems with the kids. "They were all dynamites. Then I came along, who knew all their mothers. If they didn't behave, I would call their mothers. They'd sit there like little angels."

Over the years, Bea was a eucharistic minister and lector at St. Clare's. She belonged to a scripture study group and has tried to help those in need. "It's important for us to take care of each other. It's easy to just hibernate and not pay attention, but the other people are part of our lives, too."

Bea said she tries to be open-minded about people of other faiths. "I never condemn anybody for their religion or what they believe. But people who celebrate Christmas, put up a tree, and give presents and never go to church bother me. I tell them right out, 'What are you celebrating? If you're not celebrating Christ's birthday, what's the point?' I don't care if you don't believe. I'm just saying you can't be a hypocrite."

Deolinda Avila is convinced of God's influence in her everyday life. When she wrote her Azorean cookbook, it was divine inspiration that got her started. "I feel like it was the Holy Spirit who inspired me really, because I had been helping with the Holy Ghost celebration."

She had been in Portugal the summer before and thought about the need for an Azorean cookbook. She started writing her book for the Holy Ghost festival, planning to give copies away. Everything came together: traveling to Portugal, shopping for cookbooks, watching the older women cook. "Life is that way. Things happen in your life that you might not understand, but there's a reason for everything. A power up above was preparing you for the right moment. I do believe it was someone up above that gave me the courage and the strength."

Deolinda has sold more than 22,000 copies of *Foods of the Azores Islands,* and the book is still in demand. People from all over the United States write to share recipes and thank her for preserving the dishes from the old country for them.

The Holy Spirit was with her again, Deolinda said, when it came time to remodel the Portuguese hall in Mountain View. She had just taken a real estate course and had become the first woman secretary in her lodge. Her knowledge helped her work out the construction loan and handle the paperwork. She's certain the Holy Spirit guided her in that direction. Deolinda continues to be active in her church, too. She is a eucharistic minister and takes communion to elderly shut-ins.

Church is also a major part of Mary Pasqual's life. She serves as a eucharistic minister, lector, and cantor and is a member of the altar society, which provides fresh flowers for the altar. Her husband, a genius with wood, built the new altar for St. Clare's church and refurbished the stations of the cross. Along with her other ministries, Mary sings in the choir. She says she has an average voice, but "if you don't keep singing, your voice disappears. God takes care of everybody's voice; when it all blends in, it's fine."

As with Americans of all nationalities, the church plays a smaller role in many modern Portuguese American women's lives. "Religion was definitely a big part of my life, but I was not very religious," Goretti Silveira admitted. Her father wasn't active in the church. "The only person who ever read to me was my grandmother, and she read to me out of the Bible. I was the only one who would listen to her." She laughed. "The highlight of the week for Grandma was going to church."

Her grandmother took some of the Revelation stories literally. Her father told her not to pay attention, but, said Goretti, "We prepared for the end of the world a couple of times. With candles and the whole thing. The end of the world, not just a big war, but the end. First there were going to be forty days of darkness. We prepared for that."

Cristina Mendonsa's grandmother was the spiritual leader in the family. "She gave me every rosary I ever owned," she said. Today, Cristina and her husband are both Catholic. "I can't say I'm a great Catholic. I don't attend as much as I should. But I've gone through all the sacraments, and I believe."

In Sylvia Carroll's family, all the children were baptized as Catholics and had their First Communion, but none were confirmed, and they rarely attended mass. She isn't sure why they didn't have a closer relationship with the church, but she was aware that her mother and aunt didn't agree with the church's teachings. Her mother was a feminist; perhaps she saw that women worked harder and had fewer rights than men and partly blamed the church, Sylvia said. Whatever the cause, "There were no rosary beads in that family."

Zelia Escobar Naman went to Catholic schools and even attended a Catholic university for her law degree. Her parents were very religious. They went to mass every Sunday and did no work on that day. However, as an adult, she doesn't go to church much. Sometimes when parents push too hard, the children go the other way, she said. She might go more regularly when she has children, she added.

IN LOUISE PITTA POLSKY'S family, the kids went to church, but because her father had been married before, the parents stayed away. "My father tipped his hat when he went by," she said. After her father died, her mother started going to mass again.

Louise married a Jewish man and became fascinated by the Jewish culture and especially by the history of Portuguese and

Spanish Jews, sometimes referred to as Sephardic Jews. During the Spanish Inquisition in the fourteenth and fifteenth centuries, these Iberian Jews were persecuted by the Catholic Church, which dominated the area. They were forced to flee to other countries to keep practicing their faith. In fact, the first Portuguese settlers in what was to become the United States were Jews who arrived in New Amsterdam in 1654. Those who remained in Portugal were forced to at least pretend to embrace the Catholic faith. These New Christians, as they were called, were baptized, often with new names, and adopted the Christian customs. Some reverted to Judaism when they reached a safe place, while others retained their new religion and passed it down to their descendants.

Louise met and married her husband in England. When she notified her family of her wedding plans, her mother wrote back, "Do not worry about the religion." Louise, who is still a practicing Catholic, has wondered since then if maybe there was a Jewish connection in her family. When her husband was alive and they attended Jewish events, people always assumed she was Jewish, too. Louise, who is active in a Jewish genealogy society as well as researching her own Portuguese roots, believes there may be Jewish ancestors in her past.

Portuguese Protestants also fled to America to escape religious persecution. In the 1830s, Dr. Robert Reid Kalley, a missionary for the Free Church of Scotland, which later became the Methodist Church, converted hundreds of Madeirans to his faith. His fledgling church in Funchal was mobbed by angry Catholics and persecuted by civil and church authorities. The missionary and approximately 400 followers fled to the West Indies. Several hundred Madeiran Protestants subsequently moved to the United States, mostly to New York and Illinois, with the help from American church groups.

Today, non-Catholics are allowed to practice their faiths in peace, and Protestant churches are scattered throughout Portugal. However, they are still a minority in a country that remains overwhelmingly Catholic.

THE AZOREAN CULTURE is loaded with superstitions, many of them oddly tied up with their religion. Their almost cultlike devotion to the Virgin Mary is an example.

Jane Rose is convinced that she and an assistant at her fitness salon had a vision of Mary. Every day around four p.m., sunlight came through the cathedral windows of the salon, creating rainbows on the walls. One day, when business had hit a low point, she and her assistant, Rena, had a vision.

"We were sitting there, just the two of us. Light hit the chandelier, and the room was full of rainbows. All of a sudden, I looked up and saw the Blessed Mother. It's true. She was standing, just as you see her in statues up on her throne. I looked down at Rena, and she caught my eye and looked up, and we just could not speak. I mean, it was the most incredibly beautiful sight. We both stood here and sighed, and I said, 'This is beyond you and I, this really is. This business will go on in spite of us.'"

In the Azores, children are taught to fear ghosts and the evil eye. Nazaria Soares said it is common to think ghosts come back because they died without clothes on and want to steal clothing from someone who is still alive. When two people say the same thing at the same time, they need to touch something black right away. Then they will get their wish, Nazaria said. Many believe that when things are going well, one should never grow complacent or acknowledge how wonderful things are. For sure, something bad will happen.

When I was a child, my grandmother would tell my brother and me that the bogey man was right outside our house waiting to get us. Grandma was a kind woman, but she placed many fears in our impressionable minds. When storms brought thunder and lightning, she told us God was angry; Mom countered that it was just the angels bowling.

Edith Walter's mother-in-law, Rita Lewis, had lots of fears. Rita's son would not ride a taxi because of the dire things she said would happen to him if he did. Rita herself would never go out without clean underwear or wear her underpants inside out. The one time

Rita went without, she was in an auto accident and wound up going backwards over the seat; she landed with her feet straight in the air and everything exposed. Trying to reassure her, Edith said, "It probably wasn't the first time they've ever seen it." "First time they saw me!" Rita replied.

Rita would throw salt over her shoulder and wouldn't walk on a crack. She believed dreams were omens. If she dreamed of killing pigs, there would be a death. If she dreamed about a wedding, she would hear bad news.

Portuguese Pioneers of the Sacramento Area tells the story of Maria Silveira Bittencourt. She was a lonely woman who stuttered badly and was mistreated by her husband. Her neighbors called her a *feiticeira*, a witch. "She would mix potions and try to cast spells upon people she knew. She became quite superstitious and actually believed she had the power to bewitch, perhaps to cover up her loneliness and mistreatment.

"One witchcraft effort that took place in Maria's home was experienced by one of her young neighbors, Anna Soto. Anna and some young friends stopped by to visit Maria Bittencourt one afternoon. She regarded Anna as a nice young lady from a nice family, a desirable candidate upon whom to cast a spell to lure her into marrying her youngest son, Joe Bittencourt.

"The young ladies had entered through the back door, which in country homes was always the main entrance, and then were invited to sit in the parlor. After some conversation, suddenly there appeared, much to Anna's horror, a freshly spread white powdery chalkline across the parlor floor beginning near Anna's chair. No one saw how it got there. Anna became frightened and knew immediately that she was not to cross over that white line. However, in a flash, she got up, turned around, and made a sudden exit through the rarely used front door. She vowed never to return to that house again."

Sandra Wolforth tells stories given to her by two Provincetown, Massachusetts, women in 1974. Certain "old women" were said to have special powers. A child had been ill for a long time. An old woman was called in who sprinkled garlic, pepper, and little sticks around the child's bed. When the child recovered, they believed it was because of the old woman's efforts. Wolforth also describes Tia Rita from Provincetown. She was seen performing an exorcism of a woman with cancer, using a crown and crucifix, and burning human hair and nail parings.

The early immigrants believed in special cures for various illnesses. Epileptics were to travel to Georgia, have sugarcane cut by a black thirteen-year-old child, then burn the cane and bury it. For a fever, one should wear a garlic necklace. As the garlic shriveled, the fever disappeared.

Jane Rose said her grandmother was a shaman. She would concoct all sorts of potions to heal illnesses and injuries. Jane loved to watch her work. Her grandmother also told fortunes, but only on Catholic holy days. She would take a glass of water and a straw from a broom, dip the straw in olive oil, then let a drop of the oil fall into the water. The shape the drop took showed the person's fortune.

"Superstitions also dealt with the happier aspects of life," Wolforth writes. "On St. John's Day, June 24, a young woman should throw a basin of water out her window. The first man to step in the puddle would give the girl his name. However, if a woman stepped in the puddle, the girl would remain unmarried. One of the women in Provincetown claimed that this worked for her because the man who stepped in the puddle she had thrown had the same first name as her future husband.

"Minor superstitions abounded in Portuguese folklore. Children had to wear a necklace with a hand, a heart, a cross, and a horn to protect them from evil. Evil spirits could be warded off by forming a "*figa*," holding the thumb between the second and third fingers. One should spit at a dead dog, rat, or cat in order to keep its evil spirit away. The belief that evil spirits did exist and were capable of harming humans necessitated countless methods of evasion, few of which had any connection with organized religious practices."

Wolforth also found that women were not allowed on board fishing boats because they were considered bad luck. "This association between women and bad luck extended into a belief by many older Portuguese that real, active witches, known as *bruchas,* existed who were capable of immense evil."

Francis Rogers tells of other superstitions: "After you go to a funeral, you may not visit anyone on the way home (or else that person may also die). Or, the first time you visit someone's house, you must leave by the same door through which you entered (otherwise you remove the good luck already present in the house). Or, if a girl is particularly anxious that a certain boy be attracted to her, she solicits the aid of a witch, who in turn puts items into the boy's food or drink such as to cause him to fall in love and marry the girl."

In *Azorean Folk Customs,* Cecilia Cardoza Emilio describes other rituals designed to win a sweetheart. "In Terceira, it is very popular for a girl to cut up as many little slips of paper as there are boys for whom she has an amorous interest. On each paper she writes a boy's name. Rolling or folding the papers, she places them in a plate of water. The plate is set out in the open air overnight. Early in the morning, before sunrise, she checks to see if one of the papers has opened up. If it has, that name is the name of her future sweetheart. If all are closed, there will be no marriage that year. If all are open, none of them will be her sweetheart. If more than one is open, the chosen name will be the one on the paper which has opened the most."

The shape of an egg, the placement of needles in water, picking fava beans and seeing which one peels, and studying snail tracks are among the other indicators of future spouses.

Most of these superstitions, both the frightening ones and the charming ones, have faded in America, although sayings remain. What Portuguese American child hasn't heard of the evil eye or been given instructions to follow a practice that makes no sense except to a superstitious *Avó* who believes in ghosts?

The early immigrants found no conflict between their superstitious ways and their devout Catholicism. The same God was in charge of everything.

8

Every Town Has a Portuguese Lodge

MARY SIMAS'S son-in-law, Ken Schlenker, shook his head, affectionately remembering her as "Crazy Mary." Several of the men in the family called her that, admitted Mary's daughter, Maree Carmen Simas Schlenker.

It was in honor of her mother that Maree spent months driving three hours each way from her Roseville home to San Jose to help prepare for the opening of the Portuguese Museum. Mary, whose parents came from São Jorge, often spoke of the need for recognition of her quiet, hard-working people. She attended the dedication of the site but died before the museum opened on June 7, 1997.

Unlike many Portuguese women who rarely left their homes, Mary Simas rarely stood still. The mother of eight, she belonged to many civic organizations. Always interested in history, she joined the O'Connor '89ers, San Jose Historical Museum Association, California Pioneers of San Jose, and the Native Daughters of the Golden West Vendome Parlor, as well as the Santa Clara Women's Club, Santa Clara Cultural Society, Santa Clara Sister City

Association, National League of American Pen Women, St. Clare's Circle of Druids, Triton Museum of Art Alliance, St. Justin's Ladies Guild, Young Ladies Institute, and the Santa Clara County planning review board. "She must have belonged to forty organizations," Maree said. At Mary's funeral, the Santa Clara Mission church overflowed with her admirers.

The Portuguese lodges were her special love. Mary belonged to the Sociedade do Espírito Santo (SES) of Santa Clara; the Cabrillo Club; Sociedade Portuguesa Rainha Santa Isabel (SPRSI); and União Portuguesa Protectora do Estado da Califórnia (UPPEC). She became interested in the lodges through her mother, Rosa Gabriel Nascimento. "Nothing could prevent Grandma from going to her lodge meetings," Maree said. Rosa and Mary both marched with the SPRSI drill teams, and Maree remembers her grandfather always donating cows for the SES *festas*.

When Mary joined a group, she was never just a member. Maree chuckled, remembering that the year her mother joined the UPPEC lodge, she became the past president, even though she had never served as president. The previous president had died, so she was happy to take her place. That's the way she was. "If she could be involved, she would. She had more energy than you could imagine."

Maree said her father also enjoyed the Portuguese activities but was often frustrated that his wife was always baking cakes to take to other people.

Mary learned to drive when she was fifty-five years old. She didn't tell anyone in the family. She secretly bought an old police car and hid it at an uncle's apartment building. One day when everyone was there, Mary asked them to come outside. To their astonishment, she got in her car and drove off.

She would need that car for her many activities. For years, Mary lived across the street from her parents' dairy on Lawrence Road in Santa Clara. After Maree finished high school, the family moved to downtown Santa Clara on Lexington Street. Even when they moved to Hollister, Mary kept coming back to town. She would drive to Santa Clara to work at a packing house, drive home to fix dinner for her husband, then drive back north for social events or for the classes she was always taking, mostly at Gavilan College in Gilroy.

In her later years, she studied writing and penned several articles on her Portuguese family and their history. The articles are now in the archives at the San Jose Historical Museum, where Mary was a docent. From a box of memorabilia she was still sorting, Maree displayed a photo of a costume Mary made with the flowers of every U.S. state embroidered on the skirt. Mary is gone, but her creations will continue to live on for future generations who visit the Portuguese museum.

"That was my mother. She had so much energy." Maree said. If people called her Crazy Mary, that was just a term of endearment.

WHEN THEY REMEMBER Aunt Nellie McKee, my parents say that her lodges were her life. Dinners, balls, and official visits kept her hopping from town to town. She had a closet full of formal gowns for lodge affairs. When she died in 1994, her lodge sisters lined up around her casket for a farewell ceremony, each saying a few words and presenting a rose.

The Portuguese lodges, both male and female, read like alphabet soup to the uninitiated. The initials usually stand for a Portuguese name that includes some mention of the Holy Spirit, *o Espírito Santo*. They began as service organizations; immigrants banded together to help each other, to raise money for the church, and to socialize. Today, every town that has more than a handful of Portuguese citizens has a lodge. They put on the *festas*, crab feeds, and scholarship dinners that bind the community in fellowship and preserve the Portuguese culture. Members march in parades, proudly carrying the lodge banner, escorting the lodge queens and officers.

One source called the Portuguese lodge the Portuguese version of the Kiwanis Club, which is a pretty fair assessment. Like the Kiwanis club, the lodges offer fellowship and service, but everything they do has a Portuguese accent.

Many of the traditional lodges were for men, with female auxiliaries. Only in recent years have the men's lodges let women join and hold office. A common thread among the lodges is insurance, with most lodges offering life and health insurance coverage to their members.

One traditionally female lodge was UPPEC. It was founded in 1901 by a group of Oakland women, led by Maria C. Leal Soares Fenn. In 1969, UPPEC began to admit men. With seventy-three subordinate councils representing an affiliation of more than 9,000 members, the Hayward-based lodge has total assets of more than $6 million and is almost 100 years old.

Marie Balshor remembers that her mother, Maria Sequeira, was an officer in the local UPPEC. Her annual vacations were the lodge conventions, held all over California. "My mother made many beautiful friends that way," Marie said.

SPRSI is one of the biggest Portuguese women's lodges, with approximately 10,000 members in 100 local councils. Based in Oakland, SPRSI sells life insurance and annuities. All members are required to sign up for the lodge's insurance. But it is also a major social outlet for many women, mostly senior citizens at this point. In addition, SPRSI supports various causes, including the Portuguese museum in San Jose and a shelter for the homeless in Oakland.

Under the leadership of Rosa M. Oliveira, the lodge was organized by thirty Portuguese women in 1898 in Oakland "to render material aid to their sisters in time of need" and as an altar society of Saint Joseph's Church. For their patroness, they chose Saint Isabel, a twelfth-century Portuguese queen who was canonized by the Catholic Church for her good deeds and charitable acts. The lodge adopted "Charity, Sociability and Protection" as their motto.

SPRSI sponsors patriotic, civic, and social activities and donates money and materials to the poor. Junior units for teens and young women sponsor their own activities. They raise money and give out scholarships annually. Once a year, they hold a youth day. In between, there are ski trips, parties, and other events for the youngest members of SPRSI. At SPRSI's annual convention in June, members choose a

The UPEC's fifteenth convention, Santa Cruz, September 17–21, 1916

queen on the basis of her fundraising efforts. She represents SPRSI in lodge parades and other events.

Marie Wilson, statewide president of SPRSI in 1992–93 and a member of SPRSI for more than fifty years, is proud that her granddaughter is due to be elected president in 1998. SPRSI seems to run in her family. "I was raised into it," Marie said. Her mother, who immigrated from Faial at age fifteen, joined SPRSI shortly after she arrived because she had heard the lodge provided assistance to families dealing with death or illness. She also belonged to UPPEC.

Marie's father was a member of Irmandade do Divino Espírito Santo (IDES) and União Portuguesa do Estado da Califórnia (UPEC). UPEC, then the largest men's fraternal organization, oversees the

Freitas Portuguese Library at its headquarters in San Leandro. It also gives money to charities, holds social events, and sells insurance.

Marie, an only child, attended the meetings with her parents; when she was old enough, she joined her mother's favorite lodge. She soon rose through the ranks, holding every local and state office. "You can say I've pretty much dedicated myself to SPRSI," said Marie.

Those who belong to one lodge tend to join others. They may join SPRSI for the insurance and the local lodge for the *festas.* Marie belongs to other lodges in the Oakland area. "They kind of rope you into it." She attends their events, but is not as involved in the other groups as she is in SPRSI.

Delia and Ludovico Mendes are active in the Sacramento Portuguese Holy Spirit Society. They helped renovate the lodge hall, which is just down the street from their home in Sacramento's Pocket neighborhood. At the *festas,* Ludovico cooks *sopas* while Delia helps in the kitchen. Ludovico was president of the lodge in the 1980s. During his term, all three of their daughters were queens in the annual Holy Ghost festival. The Mendeses also belong to UPEC and the Luso-American Fraternal Federation. They used to be members of the Portuguese Heritage and Cultural Society, but found themselves overloaded with too many volunteer activities.

Deolinda Avila is active in Mountain View's Irmandade da Festa do Espírito Santo (IFES). She was the first woman elected secretary. After her election, other women were elected director and treasurer. She got the job partly because she had taken a real estate course and could help manage the paperwork. Through her efforts, the hall was finished, and the club's non-profit status remained secure.

The board had been all-male since the lodge's founding in 1926, Deolinda said. Until she was elected in 1988, women had always been on the sidelines as part of the auxiliary. "The women worked, but they had no say." Membership opened up to women around 1980. "Since '88, women are on the board, and they've made a difference."

Deolinda has helped make the IFES known in the community by serving as a bilingual spokeswoman, particularly as a go-between for the annual *festas* and parades. "I don't know what it is, but I'm

The SPRSI on parade at the IDES convention, San Rafael, September 17, 1908

put in a position to have to deal with all the officials." After she joined the board, she invited the mayor and vice mayor of Mountain View to the *festa*. "For years, IFES was there, but they never knew what it was."

After nine years on the IFES board, Deolinda finally retired. As we talked, a bouquet from the lodge was still blooming on her table. She was worn out from all the meetings, phone calls, and fundraisers. "I don't mind helping, but I need a break."

It wasn't easy being one of the few women on the board, Deolinda admitted. Most of the leaders are men from the old country, many with only a fourth grade education. "They stopped learning," she said. Her ideas often met strong resistance. "Sometimes I wondered, 'What am I doing here?'"

Anyone can join IFES if they are of Portuguese descent or married to a Portuguese person. IFES has almost 1,000 members, including husbands, wives, and children. "It's a family thing," Deolinda said. They work on projects together, for example, cleaning sixty pounds of garlic or slicing 100 pounds of onions for lodge dinners. They sit all day, working and talking. The kids are there with them, Deolinda said. "There's a certain age that they pull away, but they come back. For a period there, you don't want to have anything to do with it."

However, the lodges are aging. Deolinda said IFES needs more young people. "They're going to have to change these organizations a lot, because we do not have the people coming from Portugal that we had. The meetings are in Portuguese, the minutes are written in Portuguese. We can have the same ideas, but go with the times and change it. There will come a time when we have to change to English and have it open to more people. With mixed marriages, we can't get new members if everything is in Portuguese."

Deolinda organized a youth group for the Mountain View IFES. They have held their own dances and fundraisers, gathering money for scholarships. The lodge has to offer something of interest to today's youth, she stressed. "Going in the parade and being the queen is not enough for these kids."

Marie Wilson said most of SPRSI's councils operate in English now, although they used to speak only Portuguese. A few councils still hold their meetings in Portuguese or a blend of both languages in an attempt to keep everyone happy. She agreed that the lodges need to adapt to attract young members. "You've got to have a really interesting program to get them to give up their time."

Mary Ann and Lucille Cabral both belonged to lodges, mostly as part of the Holy Ghost *festas*. Mary Ann joined SES and SPRSI, and Lucille belonged to IDES. They always attended the celebrations when they were young. Now they are still members but don't want to get involved in committees and lodge projects.

Bea Costa belongs to several Portuguese organizations. "You can't miss it if you're Portuguese and in business." She's a past president of the UPEC council. Her children also joined UPEC. Her daughter was fraternal director, and her son-in-law was supreme director. Bea's son joined the lodge but was more active in Lions, Elks, and other groups. Although Bea belongs to the Portuguese lodges, she prefers more general organizations, such as Soroptimists, and has been active in Santa Clara civic groups.

Lorraine Freitas's father and uncle were officials in Associação Protectora da União Madeirense do Estado da Califórnia (APUMEC), a group dominated by immigrants from Madeira. She joined when they let women in, but said, "I don't want to be supreme president. That's just not my cup of tea." It used to be that the fraternal organizations would help each other out. "Now everything is fraternal insurance." They still host community events, but it's more of a business, Lorraine said. She was chair of the board for APUMEC and oversaw the construction of the office in Hayward.

"They usually find one sucker and work them to death. That's in every organization. They will find maybe three good workers who will do everything," Lorraine said. She got tired of it. They used to meet at the SES hall in Santa Clara. Members would give people rides to the meetings, set up the tables, and clean up afterward.

When APUMEC was strictly men, they would come to her house, tell her mother they wanted her to do the cooking, then ask Lorraine to help serve the food. Her dad was involved with the lodge through St. Anthony's kitchen. She and her mother would work hard hauling big pans of meat and bread there. "I'm glad that I've grown up. You couldn't say no. There was no such word as 'no' to them."

Today, there are fewer Portuguese immigrants, and the lodge members are aging. "There's a lot of older people," Lorraine said. "The young people don't want to become involved. They have too many outside interests, and a lot of them don't care. Someday they'll be sorry that they didn't continue on with their traditions, but it's gotten to the point now that these organizations are beginning to suffer."

Mary Pasqual, who came to the United States from Faial when she was three years old, belongs to more organizations than she can count, but each one has added something to her life. Her mother was active in SPRSI, and Mary followed suit, becoming an officer in that organization. "We had wonderful times with those ladies," she said. But she is worried about the future of the lodge. Most of the women are elderly. Quite a few have died, and their numbers are dwindling. The local group no longer meets every month.

One by one, the lodges founded in the days of the largest Portuguese immigration are coming up to their 100th birthdays. SES in Santa Clara, for example, was formed in 1896 to feed the poor and the hungry. People still meet at the lodge at Lewis and Lafayette streets for dinners, dances, and the annual *festas*.

SPRSI held a grand celebration in Oakland for its centennial in March 1998. Marie Wilson chaired the event. Activites included banquets, installation of officers, a bay cruise, and a centennial dinner at which the women were asked to dress in turn of the century garb. Because the annual convention, usually held in July, was combined with the centennial, the women of SPRSI planned a trip to Portugal in July 1998 to attend the feast of their patron Saint Isabel on the mainland, then visit Madeira and the Azores.

While technically not a Portuguese lodge, the Young Ladies Institute, which started as a church altar society, draws many Portuguese women, most of them no longer young. Mary Pasqual joined in 1948 and has been an officer ever since; she is re-elected secretary every year. Mary worked her way up from local involvement to become 1974–75 grand president of the organization. That year she traveled to approximately 130 different institutes, including YLIs in Washington, Oregon, California, and Hawaii.

The YLI links many Portuguese women in the Bay Area. Mary named a Who's Who of Portuguese women in Santa Clara and nearby cities who belong to YLI. Nellie McKee introduced her when Mary became grand president of YLI. She knows Edna Sousa and many other old-time members. But she has participated in too many lodge farewell rites at members' funerals. "Practically all the ladies I knew that were so dedicated and involved, they're all dead. It's kind of sad—all the people that we loved so much and had such good times with are gone."

The YLI, like most of the other lodge-type organizations, is not attracting many young women. Membership is down to about half what it was when she joined, Mary said. "Society has changed so much; young women don't have time to go to work and take care of a family and do all the things that you have to do now in order to survive." Women are more active in the lodges in the rural areas, but not in the metropolitan areas. "We have too many things to do in the city."

There are those who criticize the lodge ladies for being away from home a lot, Mary admitted, but she credits her lodge and YLI memberships with many of the best experiences of her life, including traveling to the Holy Land, the British Isles, Rome, and all over the United States. "The organizations that I belonged to opened doors to things that I would never have had open to me if I hadn't been involved."

Her husband, Ed, is a past president of the Young Men's Institute, YLI's male counterpart, but is not as active as Mary. "He doesn't get involved in organizations like I do," she said, "but he has never told me I couldn't belong to anything or do anything. In fact, he's the one that helps me with a lot of the things that I do." As for those who scoff, "They don't understand the bond that you experience when you join these organizations because you meet people from all over."

The organizations also contribute to society. In YLI, every grand president chooses a special cause. Mary's program was literacy. She told people how her father never learned to read or write, how she used to help him get his driver's licenses and handle his business papers. People donated books, volunteered as tutors, and worked in libraries as part of her program. Past presidents have focused on cancer, guide dogs for the blind, Special Olympics, and Alzheimer's disease. In addition, YLI supports future priests by contributing money to the seminaries. Over the years, members have donated more than $2 million. "We do a lot of good," Mary stressed.

9

I'm Proud to be Portuguese

 WHEN BEA COSTA talks, it's pure New Jersey. Even though she works in a sausage factory, walking among pungent racks of *linguiça* and chorizo all day, under the sweatshirt that keeps her warm in the big freezers, she wears a stylish pants outfit and matching earrings. Her gold and white hair is beauty-parlor perfect, as are her makeup and pink fingernails—no black-garbed Portuguese matron here.

Working the counter at Neto Sausage Factory in Santa Clara, Bea greets every customer as a friend and is happy to stop for a cup of coffee and a chat at one of the little tables covered with red-checked cloth. Her family says she spends too much time talking to customers, but she believes it's an important part of the job. "They become friends, just like part of my family." Sometimes they need someone to talk to as much as they need a pound of *linguiça*, she added.

Bea is American-born, but her heritage is 100 percent Portuguese, and she's proud to tell anyone who asks. Her father grew up in continental Portugal, in the northern town of Chaves, close to the Spanish border. Her grandfather was a border guard. Bea's husband, Manuel, was born in São Miguel.

As she was growing up, there was little question that Bea would work in the food business. After her parents immigrated to New York, her father started working with a Spanish man who made chorizo. Then he met a Portuguese man in Jersey City who made Portuguese sausages; soon her father was in the sausage business. Years later, when Bea and her husband decided to move to California, the whole family went with them. In 1947, her father bought a small restaurant in Oakland, but he soon went back to sausages, opening his shop in Santa Clara. Although his name was Gomes, he called the shop Neto after the name his family used for him when he was a little boy.

There was no competition then. Now several other companies in the Santa Clara Valley sell Portuguese sausage, but Neto has thousands of loyal customers who have been shopping there for generations. Bea's family has its own secret *linguiça* recipe, a magic combination of spices that make Neto sausages distinct.

When her father got older, Bea and her husband ran the business. She did the books, worked behind the counter, and made sausages in the back room. "I twisted *linguiça*; I packed it to ship out; I've done the books; I've done all kinds of stuff that needs to be done." As the business grew, so did the shop. The family kept buying more land and adding more rooms until now the Costas own most of the block.

Although Neto sells mostly sausage and a variety of other imported Portuguese foods, it also stocks many items from Latin America. A new country feels less strange, Bea said, when people can find the foods they used to eat at home.

Being in the Portuguese sausage business, the Costas can't help being involved in the Portuguese community. Bea belongs to all the lodges. These days, however, her children are more involved in Portuguese activities than she is. Her commitments have moved into the community at large. She is a Soroptimist, has served on the

Citizens Advisory Committee for the city of Santa Clara, and has been a docent at the Triton Museum.

For years, she was a volunteer at her children's school and was often called on to translate for Portuguese families. She once went to the Central Valley to be a go-between in a union dispute between employers and Portuguese employees of a large food-processing company. She also worked as an ombudsman at O'Connor Hospital. "If you can help people, it's important," she said.

She is very active at St. Clare's Church, where she has taught catechism, served as a Eucharistic minister and lector, and worked in various church groups. One of her projects has been helping the homeless. "It's important for us to take care of each other. It's easy to just hibernate and not pay attention, but the other people are part of our lives, too."

Bea and Manuel's son, Ed, and their daughters, Mary and Susie, run the shop now. Bea still comes to work when they need an extra hand because she enjoys being around people.

Bea is proud of what her children have done with the business. Ed handles the manufacturing and wholesale marketing. Most of the pizza parlors in the county buy their sausage from Neto, Bea boasted. Her daughter Susie takes care of the books, and Mary looks after the deli and catering sides of the business.

"My children are all good," Bea said. "They've been in here since they were little. Now my husband retired and says, well they can take over. They've been working here all their lives, so they know what it's about."

These days, she spends a lot of time babysitting the youngest of her seven grandchildren. She loves to tell them tales of the old days before VCRs and refrigerators and thinks someday she might publish some of the stories and poetry she writes.

Although completely Americanized, Bea is glad to acknowledge her Portuguese roots. "I was always proud to be Portuguese. I still am. As a matter of fact, I tell everybody they should be. If they haven't been to Portugal, they should go and see the country and be proud of their heritage."

Bea often leads tours for schoolchildren though the sausage factory. She guides visitors through the maze of rooms, unfazed by the noise, the smells, or the sudden temperature changes from oven hot to freezer cold. She never tires of telling the story of the little business that has grown through three generations. At the end of the tour, she wraps up a couple sticks of *linguiça* in butcher paper. "Here, take some home for breakfast," she says. "And come back and see me again. Okay?"

 SAN JOSE City Councilmember Margie Fernandes didn't grow up conscious of her Portuguese roots, even though she was surrounded by Portuguese Americans in her home town of San Leandro. It was not until she became a councilmember in a city with a large Portuguese population that she reconnected with her ancestors.

In fact, when she planned a family vacation in 1989 to Koloa, Hawaii, she had no idea it was the same city that her paternal grandparents, immigrants from São Miguel, had left for the mainland exactly 100 years earlier after working on the sugarcane and pineapple plantations. After her father explained the connection, Margie, her husband Paul, and their five children explored their family history, visiting the church her grandparents had attended and touring the cemetery full of Portuguese names.

"Because my mother was Irish, I was not brought up in the Portuguese culture," said Margie, whose maiden name was Matthews, an Americanization of Mateus. She and her six brothers and sisters were familiar with the food and the *festas*. Her grandfather Frank Matthews was president of UPEC lodge's Oakland council in 1902, but her parents and grandparents spoke mostly English and strove to blend in with the American society.

It was sheer coincidence that Margie married a Portuguese man, she said. They had met when she was fifteen and he was seventeen, courted through their years in high school, and married young. "He was cute," said Margie. "I didn't realize until later that all Portuguese men are cute."

Margie and Paul Fernandes have five children, and the future councilwoman spent most of her young adulthood raising them. However, she was determined to get a college education. "I set a course to stay in school. It took me twelve years to get my BA (political science, California State University, Hayward) and nine years to get my master's (history, San Jose State University)." After graduation, she taught English-as-a-second-language classes, working with immigrants from all over the world, including Portugal.

Margie had always been a leader. In addition to her teaching, she served on the city's parks and recreation commission, on a city commission studying the Japanese internment during World War II, and on various volunteer boards. She also worked on former mayor Tom McEnery's campaign. Her interest in politics led to a job as an aide to Susan Hammer, who was then the councilmember representing downtown San Jose. Margie was still teaching and raising her family.

Finally, in 1992, she ran for city council, becoming the first Portuguese American to serve on that body. "I've always been attracted to government, even at St. Leander's. I was president of the eighth grade. I was sort of bossy," she said, chuckling.

Her position has put her in contact with the Portuguese community. The Berryessa district that she represents has a large Portuguese population. She is also the council liaison for the Portuguese Museum and is a frequent guest at Portuguese dinners and special events.

"I'm so happy to have reconnected with the Portuguese here in San Jose," she said. "I feel real comfortable, even though I don't have a history with them. I really like them." Her husband, Paul, a Piedmont Hills High School teacher, was raised in the Portuguese tradition. "My husband just beams. He really likes to go to Portuguese events."

Margie said she is pleased with the success of the Portuguese Chamber of Commerce and other local groups working to preserve Portuguese culture. "It gives me a sense of personal pride. I'm glad that the Portuguese community here in San Jose is getting more visibility and taking their rightful place along with all the other cultural groups."

EDNA SOUSA'S mother and aunt used to sit on the front porch talking for hours. Edna was embarrassed. "I told my mother and my aunt not to speak so loud so people wouldn't know we were Portuguese." Her sister, Virginia Silveira, refused to speak Portuguese once she started school. Edna and Virginia grew up in a time when Portuguese Americans were subject to the same discrimination as blacks, Mexicans, and other minorities.

Most Portuguese are Caucasians, but immigrants from the Azores, Madeira, and continental Portugal were often lumped into the same category as the black immigrants from the Cape Verde Islands, a former Portuguese colony off the west coast of Africa. People labeled them as black and thus inferior.

In *The Portygee*, written in 1920 by Joseph C. Lincoln, the main character's American boss uses that term as a derogatory label for all foreigners. "Spanish, Portuguese, African, I don't know or care," he says. When the unfortunate worker falls in love with the boss's daughter, the romance ends in tragedy because he's a "Portygee." *Cranberry Red*, a 1938 novel by Edward Garside, depicted the Portuguese as simian, simple-minded, lustful carousers. The men were lazy, and the women were loose. *Murder on Cape Cod* by Frank Shay showed the Portuguese main characters as gorilla-like and stupid, while the newspaper *Time and the Town* alleged that several Provincetown families were black *bravas* from Cape Verde "passing" for white. Even so-called scholarly pre-World War II works implied that the Portuguese were less intelligent than people from other parts of Europe.

With popular culture painting the Portuguese in negative terms, many second-generation Portuguese Americans strove to divorce themselves from their Iberian roots. Virginia Silveira remembered overhearing a friend's mother talking about her: "This little girl lives down the street. She's Portuguese, but they're really nice people, just like white people." Virginia shook her head. "My God, if I told my mother that, she'd have gone down there with an ax."

She was angry when people denigrated her sister. "It's just hysterical to look back and think anybody would call Edna black Portuguese," Virginia said. "Edna had blue eyes and very fair skin. It was laughable, but then I grew up with 'dagos, wops, and kikes' and you don't hear that anymore."

Elaine Avina Fagalde said she was the only Portuguese youth she knew growing up in the Rose Garden area of San Jose. She still gets upset remembering the high school teacher who referred to the Portuguese people as the "brown race." "That made me so mad. I was whiter than she was."

Mary Machado compared the Portuguese in the 1920s and 1930s to the recent wave of Southeast Asian immigrants, who are the latest group to face resentment and discrimination.

Marie Balshor grew up in Dixon, a farming community in the Central Valley. "In a small town, it was not easy being Portuguese. We were kind of looked down upon, I'm sorry to say. I had a mother that didn't speak any English. I had to struggle and fight for everything I wanted, like being in the school play or being May queen or even being the Holy Ghost queen. Everything was a struggle, but I think I'm a better person for having experienced all that."

When Mary Cabral O'Reilly married into an Anglo family, she got the impression her mother-in-law thought her son was marrying beneath his class. She always felt her husband wanted her to downplay her Portuguese heritage.

A child calling her a black Portagee got Mary Ann Cabral into a fight on the school bus. Where she lived in Tracy, all the children were either "Okies" or "Portagees." "They called us black Portagees," Mary Ann said. "Well, I made a statement I should never have made, but I gave them my honest opinion. We had a fight on the bus, all the Okie kids against the Portuguese kids. The girl shouldn't have called me a black Portuguese because I'm not. I'm not dark. I told her, I don't think that's fair, you being prejudiced against us. I am American, but I'm of Portuguese descent. I was born here. So where did your family come from?"

Doris Machado Van Scoy found out she didn't get into a sorority in college because she was Portuguese. That was not the official reason they gave her, but a girlfriend found out the truth.

Others deny ever experiencing discrimination. Eva Gomes said, "We were American. We never felt like a minority."

Her daughter, Donna Gomes Austin, was quick to protest. "I did! Why didn't you teach me Portuguese then? You guys didn't teach us because you didn't want us to be different. Why did Daddy make us wear long-sleeved shirts to the beach? Why, because he didn't want us to get dark."

Pauline Correia Stonehill overheard comments about "damned Portagees" and "black Portagees" while she was student teaching in Oakland. She got a kick out of surprising people by announcing that she was Portuguese. Tall, with fair skin and auburn hair, she didn't fit the stereotype at all.

Patricia Borba McDonald could pass for Irish or Greek or any of several other nationalities, she said. "You can't always tell a Portuguese person by looking at her. We recognize each other, but it's harder for other people unless we're in a group."

When Bea Costa was in high school, someone asked her if she was Greek. "I said, 'I'm not Greek; I'm Portuguese.' They said they thought all Portuguese were black. I said, 'Look how you learn something new every day. We are white. There are black people in America, but all Americans aren't black. If you knew history and paid attention in school, you would know Portuguese have colonies that have black people, but the continent and the islands are all Caucasian people.'"

Portuguese American parents counseled their children to ignore the discrimination and not to discriminate against others. "The same God who made you made her," Lorraine Freitas's mother told her when she came home with tales of harassment leveled at a black co-worker.

"The Portuguese don't discriminate," Lorraine said. In the agricultural community where she grew up, Italians, Portuguese, Japanese, and other nationalities labored together. "Everybody was too busy working and making a living."

Whether or not they believed in their hearts that all people were the same, many Portuguese Americans strove to disassociate themselves from the Cape Verdean *bravas* and from their own Portuguese heritage, struggling to look and sound American. Some families went so far as to change their names to avoid discrimination: Pereira became Perry, Ribeira became River. And sometimes the discrimination they felt was more economic or cultural than ethnic.

Like many Portuguese American women, Amy Moody grew up on a dairy farm. The other kids never said anything, but they lived in houses, and she lived on a farm. Her parents didn't come to school events. The children ran the household because they knew English better than their folks did. Her family didn't go on vacation, didn't eat at McDonald's, didn't do the things other families did. "You think you're not different, but you are," she said.

Goretti Silveira, who came to the United States as a teenager, said, "Someone asked me if I was Mexican. I said no, I was Portuguese, and that person proceeded to apologize. There was nothing to apologize for."

Language and cultural barriers remain despite Goretti's extensive education and professional success. "I will be with some of my colleagues, and they will be referring to things of their youth that I don't have the slightest idea about, and they'll laugh. I can't laugh because I don't know what they're talking about. Sometimes people interpret that as ignorance."

Edith Walter, a docent at the San Jose Historical Museum, said her peers there didn't know she was Portuguese until the museum started working on a program to honor Portuguese contributions to the area's history. "They were surprised when I said I was full-blooded Portuguese. People thought the Portuguese were all ignorant farmers or something. I reminded them every immigrant group started out uneducated."

ALTHOUGH PORTUGUESE AMERICANS make up a large ethnic group within the United States, they shun the label minority and rarely ask for special government assistance, affirmative action, or other types of attention.

"They're very proud people," Bea Costa said. "They never want to ask for anything." Someone from the state government once asked her if the Portuguese people needed any help. "I said I don't really know if they do, because the Portuguese people, they come, and they work, and they're quiet about it. They save their money, they buy a house, they buy what they need, and they don't make a big thing about it. Not too many go on welfare or ask for food stamps or any of that. It's like a pride thing. And they kind of help one another in a quiet way, so it's a lot different."

In 1980, Father Charles Macedo, then pastor at Five Wounds Church, told the *San Jose Mercury News*, "Our people are very conservative. They are industrious people. They come over here, and they don't want to be on welfare. They'd take any kind of a job. They want to be self-sufficient, independent. That's the pride of the Portuguese people."

Mary Pasqual scoffed at the idea of giving special privileges to Portuguese Americans. "I can't see that. We never used to think of going on welfare or anything like that." She cited a San Jose community service organization that caters to the Portuguese. "My God, they get all kinds of things from the government, and they think they're entitled to it. But the whole society has changed."

While the older generations dismiss the notion of being a minority, Goretti Silveira conceded, "Yes. We are a language minority.

From an educator's point of view, I feel that students should benefit from extra services in tutoring." She also favors scholarships for Portuguese students, but cautioned, "I don't believe in special allowances of any kind." She understands why there are quotas, but is upset when they seem to cause people to hire employees with inferior skills.

In her book, *The Portuguese in America*, Sandra Wolforth writes that the newer immigrants can see the economic and educational advantages offered to minority groups that gain official governmental recognition. But the established Portuguese, who made their own way, "shun government aid and political pressure in favor of self-help and hard work. They do not wish to be considered special or an ethnic group or a minority. They have been traditionally non-militant and individualistic, never using organizations to advance their cause." She added, "The Portuguese jingoism of the newer arrivals jars the conservative Portuguese Americans who have established and maintained a record of total commitment to the American way of life."

One of those newer immigrants, Delia Mendes, smiled when asked if being Portuguese sets her apart from other Americans. "I think it's kind of neat," she said. Delia, who left her home in Pico over thirty years ago, only recently became a United States citizen. The red tape involved in holding jobs in the U.S. and traveling back to the Azores every few years forced her and her husband to do it. "I didn't want to because I didn't want to give up my Portuguese citizenship."

While in the past, immigrants worked to look, sound and feel American, ethnic pride has become increasingly popular. Second, third, and fourth generation Portuguese Americans now wish they had preserved the language and culture of their grandmothers and great-grandmothers.

They are proud of what their ancestors accomplished through hard work and determination. They may have been uneducated farmers or laborers, but their sons and daughters went to school and are teachers, doctors, and business owners. At the same time, they maintained strong family values, devotion to their church, and a deep-seated work ethic. They passed on crafts, music, food, and traditions which their descendants still treasure today.

The Portuguese were long treated as second-class citizens in San Diego, Mary Giglitto said. The builders of the San Diego Yacht Club evicted a Portuguese family to clear the land to build the club, then wouldn't accept Portuguese people as members. Today, however, the Portuguese are equal and important members of the San Diego community, honored for the large part they play in the fishing industry and for their historical contributions. Mary is president of the Portuguese Historical Center and president emeritus of the Cabrillo Festival, which both work to preserve the Portuguese culture in San Diego.

Each year, the Cabrillo Festival honors the memory of Portuguese explorer João Cabrilho, better known as Juan Cabrillo to most Californians. Cabrillo was the first European to explore the west coast of what would become the United States. During the weeklong festival, Cabrillo's landing in San Diego is re-enacted. Cabrillo and his men row ashore and land at Ballast Point, kicking off a week of symposiums, living history demonstrations, and Mexican, Portuguese, Spanish, and Native American music, dancing, and food.

As part of the festival, a Miss Cabrillo Festival is crowned. Most years, the Portuguese government invites the queen to visit Portugal; Mary goes as her chaperone and translator during their travels through continental Portugal, Madeira, and the Azores. Mary has been decorated four times by the Portuguese government and was honored by the city of San Diego with Mary Giglitto Day for her work on the Cabrillo Festival.

"I was never ashamed to be Portuguese. They work hard, are proud, earn their own way," Amy Moody said.

Cheri Mello, who is one-quarter Portuguese but has a Portuguese surname, has always told people she was Portuguese, despite her mother's insistence that she had a lot more English and Scottish in her than anything else.

On the other side of the coin, Josephine Silva, half Portuguese and half Italian, claimed a heritage she didn't even have. She didn't know anything about the Portuguese until she met her Portuguese husband. Growing up during World War II, she hesitated to say she was half Italian, because the Italians were the enemy. When she said she was Portuguese, "No one had ever heard of it." She had a Filipino friend who had dark hair and eyes like her. "I told everyone I was Filipino." She robbed herself, she says now.

"Our family was not one to hide their heritage," said Pat Silva Corbera. "We are Portuguese to this day." Although her daughter is only half Portuguese, she, too, is proud of her Iberian roots.

Deolinda Avila, who has already preserved her family's recipes in an Azorean cookbook, said she is thinking about writing a children's book about the Portuguese culture. She is anxious to preserve the traditions that came from the old country. She has put away needlework made by members of her family with notes about the history of each piece and the person who made it.

While some families never talked about the old country, Cristina Mendonsa remembers her parents and grandparents sitting around the table sharing memories. "I loved hearing them talk about their parents or the old country. We would have lots of kitchen table chats where the kids wouldn't really talk, just kind of listen. It was a lot of fun. A videotape that we still cherish is one of those kitchen table chats, where we just set up the video camera on the counter one Easter, and we all just sat around the table and talked. My mother and I love to get out this videotape and play it sometimes just because those were some of my favorite times of childhood."

Cristina remembers her family talking about an uncle who was a geologist and his travels to various countries. They would reminisce about growing up on ranches in Los Banos and Turlock and people they knew in their youth. "There were all these Portuguese names flying back and forth. It was so much more of an enclave than a community."

In her career as a broadcast journalist, Cristina has experienced more confusion than prejudice. People tend to think she is Latino.

Cristina Mendonsa, 1997

That was especially true when she worked in Colorado. Two elderly Mexican women stopped her in a grocery store there to tell her the gringos had misspelled her name, that the "s" should be a "z." No, it's Portuguese, she explained.

Cristina credits her Portuguese roots with giving her a solid identity. "I feel very secure with who I am. I can't say I feel any less American because I'm Portuguese. I'm proud mostly to be an American. My heart doesn't swell when I hear the Portuguese national anthem like it does when I hear the American national anthem. But it's a part of who I am, and I feel proud of it. I feel that my immigrant ancestors must have had very strong blood in their veins and that's where I draw my strength from. I feel strong because of all the things they did to get here. I can't imagine. They must have been very strong people, and I'm glad to have those genes and that blood."

Marie Gambrel is proud to march in Portuguese parades in the Sacramento area. She shows off costumes made in the colors of the Portuguese and Azorean flags. A framed certificate proclaiming her father's passage through Ellis Island hangs on her bedroom wall; over the bed are photos of her family. She proudly passes out copies of a recipe for Portuguese beans that was published in the *Sacramento Bee.*

The Portuguese Park installed by the Portuguese Historical and Cultural Society in Sacramento is a wonderful thing, Marie said, but she wants to do even more to commemorate her heritage. "We've just got to keep at it."

Maria Sykora is proud to be an American citizen and proud of the American traditions, but she is also proud of her Portuguese roots. She would like to see the quiet Azoreans become better known in the community. Most Americans don't even know where the Azores are. She praises the few articles that have been written about the Portuguese and wonders why Stanford, UC Berkeley, and other universities that have Portuguese studies programs don't host more Portuguese events on campus. Portuguese folkloric groups could go to schools to talk about their traditions, and more Portuguese musicians could tour in the United States. The 1997 opening of the Portuguese Museum in San Jose is a good step in the right direction, she said.

Through the generations, Portuguese women have married into other nationalities. Their children are half Portuguese and half German, French, Jewish, or Russian, and they no longer have Portuguese surnames. Patricia Borba McDonald's husband is Irish. They have tried to pass down traditions from both the Portuguese and Irish cultures, she said. "Our children are proud of both their heritages."

Josephine Silva said her grown children are not really interested in their Portuguese roots, but she plans to rebuild the connection with the next generation. "I have two grandchildren that I am indoctrinating in Portuguese."

Nellie McKee said she still thought of herself as Portuguese despite being born in California. "I'm proud to be Portuguese. If anybody asks me, I say I'm Portuguese." She added, "Don't ever let your nationality go down, whether you speak the language or not."

A SISTERHOOD of Portuguese American women has been researching their family histories, using the resources of the Mormon church and the Internet. Pat Silva Corbera started her "Journey of Discovery" in 1991 and traced part of her family story in Madeira, working with a Madeiran genealogist. Not everyone understands her quest for information about her family history, Pat said. They ask how she can understand the documents written in Portuguese, although she has only a limited knowledge of the language. "I tell them, 'My mom's sitting on my shoulder guiding my way.'"

The journey started for Pat when she found a Portuguese document among her mother's things. She took it to a Portuguese custodian at work to be translated and discovered it was her father's baptismal certificate. It contained valuable information about family members who attended the ceremony. Then, a Mormon friend took her to the temple and showed her how to use the genealogical resources there. She now knows the name of the steamship her mother came to America on and has used information about the villages her parents came from to go back sixteen generations.

Pat admits she's an Internet junkie. Her online name, Papagaia, is a family *alcunha* (nickname) used to differentiate the many Silvas in the Azores. Her grandfather used to wear a green vest, and people started calling him Papagaio, which means parrot. Pat figures that since she talks a lot, the name fits. She changed the last letter to "a" to make it female.

Another Internet fan with Madeiran roots is Louise Pitta Polsky. She is spending more and more time online, she said, tracing not only her Portuguese roots, but her husband's Jewish ancestry and the history of the Portuguese Jews. In fact, she used to like to knit, but she would rather do genealogy now. She hopes to become a certified genealogy instructor.

Paula Pimentel Hoxie is moderator for the chat room on Lusaweb, a web page for Portuguese Americans. She always wanted to know more about her heritage. Her father was 100 percent Portuguese, son of immigrants from São Miguel and Flores, but she never knew them. Her father's older sister spoke Portuguese and was interested in the Portuguese culture, but her dad would have nothing to do with it. Her aunt provided names and dates to help Paula start tracing the family's roots. "My dad never spoke of it. He never spoke the language or attended Portuguese events. We were Americans as far as he was concerned."

Donna Gomes spends hours online, especially on Lusaweb. She loves to stir controversy with questions like "What are Portuguese men really like?" She recently discovered, after living her whole life as Donna, that her birth certificate lists her as Dona with one "n." On the web, she calls herself "*Dona Gatinha,*" loosely translated as "foxy lady." Finding Lusaweb was a revelation for her, Donna said. "I felt like I found something that was home."

Much of Donna's online time is spent researching her ancestry. She has compiled scrapbooks for each side of the family. She traveled to São Miguel to trace her maternal ancestors and hopes to go to Madeira to research her father's side. It has been a slow process, one she wishes she had started when she was young. As in many Portuguese families, her older relatives never discussed their lives in Portugal or the trip to America.

"Nobody would talk about it. I'd ask my father all the time, 'What were your mom and dad like?' They didn't even know that much about them—what island they came from, what ship. If I had known what to ask then, I could have asked my grandmother, but you learn that later."

Cristina Mendonsa's mother has filled five binders with information on the family history. Always curious, Cristina's mother started asking family members questions about their history and writing down the answers. She has taken genealogy classes and recently discovered the possibilities on the computer.

Cheri Mello's interest in genealogy began when she was ten years old and assigned to do a school report on her family history. After her grandparents died, she started working on the family tree again. "The genealogy bug just bit me," she said. She started using the Internet and joined the America Online genealogy forum to help with her research. She is now the lead person for AOL's genealogy forum/chat sessions.

The Portuguese American women researching their roots work with a feeling of urgency. Every day, more of the original immigrants and their daughters die, taking with them the best source of family history. Those hardworking Portuguese women never imagined that many years later their granddaughters would be using computers to retrace the paths their families took from Portugal to America so they can proudly pass the information on to their own children and grandchildren.

10

Mothers Pass on Old-Country Traditions

WHENEVER Mary Azevedo e Melo Alves had a singing engagement, her youngest son Richard went along. He remembers all too well one night coming home over Pacheco Pass when it was so foggy the priest in the back seat never stopped praying for their safety.

Mary, founder of the choir at Five Wounds Church in San Jose, sang all her life. Not only did she lead the choir at mass, but she and others from the church took their music on the road, singing at *festas*, weddings, funerals, and other events where the Portuguese gathered. They also performed religious plays, such as dramas about the lives of saints.

In 1947, as gifts to her three sons, Mary went to the old Sherman Clay music store in downtown San Jose and recorded versions of "Ave Maria" by three different composers: Schubert, Bach-Gounod, and Renault. On the flip side of each vinyl record, she recorded a different Portuguese ballad. Today, Richard still treasures those recordings, now copied onto tape.

A native of Faial, Mary came to San Jose with her husband John S. Alves in 1910. Her husband became a barber, working at a shop at First and Bassett streets for more than fifty years. Meanwhile, Mary built her life around music and Five Wounds Church.

When Five Wounds opened in 1919, Mary Alves led the seven-member choir. She continued in that role for fifty years. One of her greatest joys was receiving a special apostolic benediction in 1961 from Pope John XXIII for her years of service to the church. Although Mary's soprano voice was untrained, it inspired those who heard it. Kay Alves, her daughter-in-law, remembers getting chills when she heard Mary sing from the choir loft.

Mary had little formal education, but she made a special effort to learn English and to pronounce the words properly, especially when she sang. Every time she heard a new word, she would write it out phonetically so she could look it up and learn it, Kay said. After Mary's death, they found her little word book among her possessions.

Mary and John Alves lived most of their lives at North Seventeenth and Empire streets, about ten blocks from Five Wounds Church. "Her whole social life revolved around Five Wounds and the Portuguese *festas,*" Kay said. Mary went to mass on Sundays but missed church during the week because she didn't drive and her husband was busy at the barber shop. John was not particularly religious, but he would go to church to socialize.

The family never had much money to spare, although Richard stressed that they always had what they needed. "My mother gave of her life what she couldn't give in money."

When she wasn't singing, Mary worked with the nuns who taught religion to the children at Five Wounds and helped new immigrants get involved in the San Jose Portuguese community. Her door and her table were always open to friends and family.

While her weekends were devoted to church and *festas,* during the week, Mary spent her days cooking, crocheting, and caring for her garden. She doted on her grandchildren and loved to babysit. The grandchildren, now grown men, wish Mary had taught them the Portuguese language. But Mary remembered all too well what happened when her oldest son, Ed, went to school not knowing how to speak English. The other kids made fun of him, so she refused to teach Portuguese to the young ones, saying it was not good for them.

She also declined to go back to her homeland, even for a visit, although her husband desperately wanted to see Faial again. When Kay and Richard visited the Azores after Mary's death, they received a warm welcome from relatives in Faial, but also saw that their parents came from extreme poverty and understood why they preferred to live in the United States.

In her final years, Mary was crippled with arthritis and had to give up the music and the social life that she loved. She died in 1971 at the age of eighty-six; John, who was ninety, died thirteen days later.

Although Mary has been gone more than twenty years, she lives on at the San Jose Historical Museum where docent Julie Pfeiffer, also a fine singer, portrays her at fashion shows and museum pageants. In 1996, the San Jose Historical Museum and the American Association of University Women, San Jose Branch, named Mary Alves as one of their Local Women of Distinction for her years of community service.

Mary's voice may continue to be heard at San Jose's Portuguese Museum, which is a replica of the Holy Ghost chapel at Five Wounds Church. The committee planning the exhibits hopes to find a way to play her three versions of "Ave Maria" for visitors to the museum.

THERE ARE TWO MARIELS.

One is a scholar. The other is a rock singer. When we first met in 1992, the Graciosa native was a student at San Jose State University, working in the foreign language office. Interview me, she said, when I came looking for a professor there. Something about this bushy-haired sprite in faded jeans, wire frame glasses, and no makeup intrigued me, so we set an appointment.

We met on a bench outside the foreign language building. It was sunny, but a brisk wind showered us with leaves and dust, and the roar of passing airplanes drowned out our voices every few minutes. Long after lunchtime, Mariel gulped down yogurt from a container. So skinny it embarrassed her, she said, "I don't like food. So I just grab something and put it in my mouth because it's a necessity."

"Are you really Portuguese?" I asked, thinking of my well-padded relatives.

"Good one," she giggled.

Both Mariels talk twice as rapidly as most other human beings. Her accent is musical, the h's often missing from the beginnings of words. On the day of our first interview, the scholar side of Mariel dominated, since she was at school, and almost nobody there knew about her other life. She spoke passionately about education, immigration laws, and politics. But the rock star emerged every now and then as she leaned closer to the tape recorder. "I want my fans to know I want them to be as happy as I am..."

A few weeks later, at a symposium, she had transformed into an academic, dressed in a dark suit, her hair in a bun, reading scholarly papers in educated English, hobnobbing with learned professors as an equal. Then, during lunch, she provided the entertainment. Off went the glasses and the plain clothes. Out came the white halter top, short black skirt, and black-on-white polka dot leggings. Her hair was loose, and her face glowed with makeup and energy as she shook her slender hips and crooned her songs with a tape-recorded backup band. Many of the songs were her own, with titles in Portuguese such as "Men on the Verge of a Heart Attack" and "Love Me or Leave Me."

The audience, mostly educated Portuguese men, admired her looks but gave a lukewarm reception to her youth-oriented music. Mariel didn't mind; the exposure was good for her career.

Now and then, Mariel measures her words, conscious of agents, record company executives, and others who worry about what she might say in public. But when she gets excited about a subject, the scholar pushes the entertainer aside to make her point and public relations considerations be damned.

The red tape surrounding immigration infuriated her. She brought her parents and one sister over from Terceira and fought with the Portuguese and United States governments for years for permission to bring the rest of her family here. She believed both governments were working together to keep Azoreans at home. "I'm for individual rights. If they want them there in the Azores, they have to make it better for them," she said.

In the Azores, those who didn't pass college entrance exams right after high school missed their chance to go to college, she said. "That's so stupid, I can't believe it. I really want to do something about that. They're still deciding who has an education and when. That's not fair."

It was the desire for education that brought Mariel to the United States in 1980. She became a citizen as soon as she could. "This country means as much to me as my country does. I'm not afraid to say it. I feel like I belong here like anybody else."

Her music career was thrust on her unexpectedly when she entered the Portuguese Festival of Song in 1991 and took first place in her district, fifth place overall. The festival was like a dream to her. She had just made her first record, mostly adaptations of Latino songs, and was performing locally when the record company entered her in the festival. Most of the other competitors had hit records and were well known.

Her time on stage is a blur in her memory, but she remembers the aftermath clearly. She was a hero in her homeland. Nobody from the islands had ever done so well. "When I got to the Azores, everybody knew who I was." Her record landed in the top twenty, and everybody loved her. "Whether I won or not, it's the same thing for these people."

Mariel, who goes by only her first name in show business, is still a big hit in the Azores. Her fans send letters and leave phone messages. Young girls ask her advice on everything from fashion to boyfriends.

She recently recorded her third album, and she spends many weekends on the road singing. Azoreans are bigger fans of her than Americans, part of which she blames on conservative radio programmers who have declined to play her music. But DJs are giving her more airplay these days, and her American audience is growing, she said.

Her target audience is teenagers, but she wants to narrow the gap between older people who were born in Portugal and their American-born offspring. Her songs reflect her inner feelings, the feelings of a young woman. "Until today, there has not been a Portuguese artist in the community that has songs for these kids, for the young," she said.

These days, when she isn't singing, Mariel teaches Spanish at Ohlone College in Fremont. She earned her master's degree at San Jose State and longs to complete her Ph.D. in the Portuguese and Spanish linguistics program at UC Santa Barbara.

The Mariel that people see is the one she chooses to project. She will not say how old she is or discuss the fact that she was once married. Nor did she mention her American-born son, now a teenager, the first time around. Her son is only fifteen but takes classes at Ohlone College. "He is my life," she said. She is putting off her doctorate because of him.

In addition to teaching and singing, Mariel is a professional translator and a certified aerobics teacher. She also sells Mary Kay cosmetics. She bought a house for herself and her son and needs more than one job to pay the bills. "I work very hard to keep us afloat, me and him."

People who know Mariel as a student or teacher are amazed to find out she's a rock singer, too. People who know only her music are surprised she is an academic. Mariel agrees that she seems like two different people, even to herself. When she dresses for a concert, she said, "I not only change in outside appearance; I change interiorly.

I have Mariel as an artist inside of me. At school, I'm a student or a teacher."

"I think Mariel as an artist has less problems. I see Mariel just being on stage. All the other problems, I give to Mariel the student or the teacher."

THE EXTENT OF Portuguese influence on everyday life depends on how far removed one is from the old country. For a fourth-generation descendant like me, the Portuguese culture was limited to a few words, occasional servings of *linguiça* and "Portagee beans," and a store of Portuguese jokes.

Repeatedly, I have found that the women whose mothers were Portuguese knew considerably more about their Portuguese heritage and traditions. When the Portuguese roots were on the father's side, they tended to disappear.

Women are the keepers of the culture. They are the ones who spend the most time with their children, who teach them their first words, feed them the ethnic dishes that become their own personal soul food, and sing them the songs that will strike a chord with them all their lives.

Katherine Vaz's mother wasn't Portuguese; she was Irish, but she valued the Portuguese traditions of her husband's homeland. She studied the Portuguese language, made sure the children attended *festas* and other Portuguese activities, and even co-wrote a Portuguese cookbook with her husband.

As nationalities become more mixed with each marriage, Katherine said she wonders what our children will be like and whether they will be interested in their roots or even be able to find them in the tangle of different heritages. "I'm wondering how our grandchildren are going to see us, their grandparents," she said.

In this all-American melting pot, it isn't easy to keep up the Portuguese traditions. Our parents struggled to seem as American as possible. Times have changed. Ethnic pride is popular, but many customs have been lost. Those who treasure their Portuguese heritage must sometimes fight to hold on to it.

Delia Mendes, an immigrant from Pico, noted sadly that her new home town of Sacramento has no stores where she can buy Portuguese food or music or crocheting supplies. She must order them from the old country or from an import house in San Jose.

Louise Pitta Polsky organizes groups of friends to attend the *festas* near her home in Southern California. She buys Portuguese CDs from the old country, and she stays in contact with Portuguese women all over the country via computer and Lusaweb.

Mary Giglitto preserves her Portuguese language and keeps in touch with the news from Portugal by watching shows broadcast by satellite from Lisbon. She tapes the soap operas for her mother, who passes them on to her aunt and uncle.

Sacramento TV news anchor Cristina Mendonsa danced the *chamarrita* as a child, but she has forgotten the steps. "I wish I remembered how to do it. I did it usually walking on top of the feet of one of my uncles. And I'm sorry that my children won't." She is part Italian on her father's side. Her mother was the one who kept them going to *festas* and dancing the *chamarrita*.

Cristina plans to find ways to share the Portuguese heritage with her kids. "I think it's going to be a lot more difficult, but I think that's just a generational thing. As the generations move along, you kind of lose touch with the language first and then you lose touch with some of the traditions, and that's sad to me because it's added so much richness to my life."

Mary Pasqual, whose children are grown, knows all too well how it goes with old-country ways. "The only tradition they keep up with is food." Her children want sweet bread every Easter, and they like to eat *sopas* and *linguiça*. Mary and her husband, Ed, used to belong to a group that performed Portuguese songs, dances, and plays, but they have dropped out. Most of their activities are not necessarily Portuguese these days, except for having *sopas* at the Santa Clara *festas*. "Maybe it's been our fault that we haven't continued to participate in the Portuguese community."

Or maybe that's the way it goes when you move to a new country. But many traditions do remain from the Portuguese culture, sometimes skipping a generation. Daughters whose mothers couldn't stand sewing pick up their grandmother's love of needlework. Mothers who cooked strictly American fare find their daughters or granddaughters asking how to make Portuguese beans. As long as Portuguese people keep immigrating to America and Portuguese Americans keep in contact with the old country in some way, the traditions will never be completely lost.

FESTA IS A religious ceremony, parade, feast, and festival all rolled into one. Portuguese *festas* honor the patron saint of a town, village, or parish, or commemorate miracles that have occurred. After the religious ceremony comes dancing, feasting, and courting among the young.

The most popular *festa* among Azorean Americans is the Holy Ghost Festival (*Festa do Espírito Santo*). Held between Easter and late fall, the *festa* honors the memory of fourteenth century Queen Isabel, a peacemaker and friend to the poor. The Portuguese believe the Holy Spirit enabled Isabel to relieve her people's suffering. According to one legend, the queen, smuggling food to the poor in midwinter, produced live roses from her robes when her husband, King Dom Diniz, demanded to see what she was concealing.

Another version of the legend says that Isabel prayed to the Holy Spirit to save her starving subjects. She promised to give up all her jewels if God would help her feed her people. When she looked up, two ships full of food were steaming up Lisbon Harbor. As she realized a miracle had occurred, she put her crown on the head of a peasant girl, fulfilling the promise she had made in her prayers. She then held a royal banquet for the poor.

The tradition is reenacted every year in the Azores and in Portuguese American communities, usually sponsored by the Portuguese lodges. Following a special mass at which a local teenage

"Little queens" at the Santa Clara Holy Ghost Festa, 1949

girl is crowned queen, the parade begins. The queens lead the march, glittering crowns on their heads, elaborate velvet capes sweeping the pavement. They are flanked by four- to six-year-old "little queens," sidemaids, signbearers, and parents. Brass bands follow, playing traditional Azorean songs and American marches by John Philip Sousa.

For the big *festas*, all the major lodges in the state send their own queens and courts to march in the parade. Following the royal court come men and women bearing baskets of bread and flowers on their heads; often, a wagon carrying a statue of Jesus or the Virgin Mary also follows.

The crowns are placed in a chapel devoted to the Holy Spirit, speeches are made, doves are released, and everyone gathers for *sopas e carne*—a soup of beef, bread, and gravy that is passed out in huge quantities for free. Then the party lets loose. They dance the *chamarrita*, sell and auction Portuguese foods and crafts, and celebrate long into the night.

In San Jose, the parade begins at Five Wounds Church and proceeds down Alum Rock Avenue to Thirty-fourth Street and back, concluding at the IES (Irmandade do Espírito Santo) Hall next to the church. More than 5,000 people attend each year. The freeway exits are blocked off for the day.

At a recent *festa* in Half Moon Bay, more than fifty volunteers cooked and served 7,200 pounds of beef, serving about 7,000 people. Luis Castro, a member of Half Moon Bay's IDES (Irmandade do Divino Espírito Santo), told the *San Jose Mercury News* the *festas*

Maree Simas Schlenker, queen of the Santa Clara Holy Ghost Festa, 1949

are a way for Portuguese Americans to maintain their culture and help the youth remember their roots. More Portuguese live outside of Portugal than in it, he noted.

Most long-time Portuguese settlers remember being involved in the *festas*. Many of the women were queens. Maree Simas Schlenker was thrilled to wear a beautiful white dress and embroidered velvet cape as queen of the Santa Clara *festa*.

The *festa* was fun for Marie Balshor, too. She was both a little queen and a big queen in Dixon. It was "wonderful, wonderful," she recalled. All summer, they traveled to Sacramento, Vallejo, Fairfield, Crockett, and other towns for the *festas*. The best part? "That's where you met the boys."

Linda Brito, who as an adult dances with a folkloric group at *festas* and Portuguese parades, was a queen at age fifteen. At seven and thirteen, she had marched as a sidemaid. "I had a ball," Linda said. She loved going to all the *festas* and parades. It was harder on her parents, who had to worry about clothing and travel arrangements for each event.

Patricia Borba McDonald carried the Holy Ghost image one year in the Mountain View *festa* parade. "I felt so important." She admired the queens and dreamed of being one, but by the time she was old enough, her family had moved to the Oakland area and were less involved in the Portuguese community.

Many report, however, that only daughters of the most influential families got to be queens and sidemaids in the Holy Ghost parades. Often the chosen girls were daughters of the lodge president or came from wealthy families. "We weren't rich enough," said Pat Silva Corbera when asked if she was a *festa* queen. Although her family always went to the *festa* and she admired the beautiful gowns and the pomp of the parade, she never had any hope of being queen.

Mary Ann and Lucille Cabral said their families would prepare special Holy Ghost dinners on their ranch and crown family members as their own queens.

Cristina Mendonsa remembers the annual *festas* for the *sopas* feed. "*Sopas* was an annual spring thing. We always looked forward to it. I can remember my other friends on the block thought it was gross, but I loved it." Although multicultural events are considered hip now, they were just part of everyday life for her family. "It wasn't like a big deal was made out of it."

Cristina was never a queen either. "I always wanted to be, but I never got to be one." She loved the parades and the dancing. "I loved just being buried in the smells and the cooking and the language. Even if I didn't understand the conversations, it felt like home."

Dolores Spurgeon got a new dress every year for the *festa*. Her family always went to the parade and the barbecue afterward. One year, her father entered her in the competition for queen. She did not want to be a *festa* queen and finally convinced him to take her name out of contention. Her older relatives probably thought she was a brat, she said. "I did carry one corner of the flag one year," she added.

Women carrying baskets of bread and flowers on their heads in a festa *parade, San Jose, 1992*

Donna Gomes Austin marched in the Santa Clara parade as a "bar girl," one of several girls carrying long poles surrounding the queen. Many years later, her daughters also were bar girls, she said. The parades always seemed terribly disorganized beforehand. "Then all of a sudden, magically, everyone gets up and they all start going."

Some families distanced themselves from the *festas* in their effort to appear completely American. Sylvia Carroll remembers a Portuguese man came to her house to refinish the piano. He told her mother that Sylvia was just the right age to be *festa* queen. Sylvia's mother drew herself up proudly and said, "Oh, we don't do that."

Edna Sousa said she would go to *festas* in both Santa Clara and East San Jose. She marched with the Young Ladies Institute drill team, but never became a queen or sidemaid because her father didn't believe in it. Besides, it would mean buying expensive gowns and going to all the *festas* in the area, including Half Moon Bay, San Francisco, and San Juan Bautista.

Nellie McKee (middle) dressed up for festa, c. *1920*

Here in the United States, families often invest large sums of money preparing their daughters for the *festa*. In the Azores, it was different, Deolinda Avila said. They didn't have crowns and capes and didn't always wear white. They would bring cows dressed up in ribbons through the villages before killing them for the celebration. The *festas* would center around the little Holy Ghost chapels called *impérios*. As in the United States, bread and meat was blessed and given to all.

Manuela Torres said the *festas* here are too Americanized. She marched in the parade in Terceira, wearing a white dress, but it was part of a religious *promessa*, not a secular affair.

Maria Sykora was asked to be a *festa* queen in Mountain View, but she declined. Not only did she not want to spend her summer attending every *festa* in the area, but she was put off by the crass practices at California *festas*. In Ponta Delgada, there was a mass and a girl carried the crown representing the Holy Spirit, but it was not "push and shove," being jammed together into a hall to eat *sopas*. It was less social and more religious. "I just got turned off by the way it was done," she said.

Delia Mendes agreed that the *festas* in the United States are not the same as at home. The current version was made in America. Her three daughters marched in the parades. She showed the eight glittery crowns her daughters have worn. The year all three were queens, they had their picture in the paper. Each marched with two sidemaids, and Delia sewed about thirty dresses that year.

Queens lead festa *march in Santa Clara, 1992*

Her daughter Yvonne said they loved being queens, although their non-Portuguese friends didn't understand. They dressed up in white dresses and capes and crowns and traveled to various towns for the *festas*.

They still have their dresses, Delia said. She wanted to send the dresses to Portugal, but her daughters wouldn't let them go. Do they have the same kinds of parades back in Portugal? Delia laughed. "No, we didn't have queens. No kings either."

For the younger generation, the *festa* highlights the clash between cultures. Many shun the idea of being queen and marching in the parade. Some are forced into it by their families. Photographed marching down a hot street, sweltering in their gowns, the girls can be seen chewing gum, wearing sunglasses, drinking Cokes, and talking to their friends, much to the disapproval of their elders.

Festas have a more traditional feel in the rural areas. In the San Joaquin Valley, where many Portuguese still operate dairy farms, thousands of people attend the *festas*. Maree Simas Schlenker said the last one she attended featured a parade of ox-drawn carts. There were also hundreds of RVs lined up everywhere they looked. Her husband Ken grumbled, "I never heard one word of English."

THE PORTUGUESE LOVE music. At every event, bands play, folkloric groups dance, and *fado* singers bring the old songs back to life. Many folkloric groups perform at *festas*, fundraisers, and other gatherings. Gui Sequeira, Delia Mendes, and other Sacramentans joined to form the Nove Ilhas folkloric group. They did traditional songs from the nine Azores islands for several shows, just singing at first, then adding a little dancing. They wore costumes that were borrowed from the Portuguese Historical and Cultural Society, given to them by the regional government of the Azores or purchased in the islands. But the most popular dances were sprightly for middle-aged dancers, and their busy schedules made it hard to get together for rehearsals. When we spoke, Nove Ilhas was in limbo, perhaps forever, Gui said, but other groups continue to preserve the traditional songs and dances.

Mention Portuguese dance and the *chamarrita* comes to mind. This Azorean specialty is a lively dance, done with a caller shouting out the steps, much like American square dancing. It is still done in California's Portuguese communities.

Elaine Almeida, who directs the Rancho Folclórico dance troupe, said her group specializes in dances from continental Portugal, but when they dance for American audiences, they always do the *chamarrita* because the audiences look forward to it. Following the Portuguese tradition, they call the audience up to dance with them.

Most of the dances are combined with songs and date back to the earlier days of singing minstrels, French troubadours, and religious pilgrimages. The songs are about every aspect of life, including love,

Folkloric dancers performing in Terceira, 1990

weather, fishing, farming, and longing for home. *Saudade*, which was first sung in the days of the fifteenth century explorers, is still sung today and reflects the homesickness of the Portuguese who left their home for America. Other dances from the islands include *O Pezinho, O Bravo, O Meu Bem, Os Olhos Pretos* and *A Sapateia.*

Many of the members of Rancho Folclórico have been performing traditional Portuguese dances since they were children. Linda Azevedo Brito started dancing at age seven in a Luso-American Education Foundation youth group. She was dancing in another group, A Portugesa, when she met her husband, Paulo, and switched groups to be with him. About a third of the twenty-four members of Rancho Folclórico are related. They include Paulo's parents and Linda's sister. Members drive from all over the Bay Area for weekly practices in Vacaville and perform at least once or twice a month. Linda said she can't do American dances but loves Portuguese-style dancing. "The dancing is a big center of who we are. I know it sounds corny, but it's a big part of our lives."

Elaine also started with a Portuguese youth dance group. When she became director of Rancho Folclórico, she started researching the Portuguese dances. On her trips to Portugal, about every four years, she buys books and music and interviews people who direct dance groups there. Many of the dances have not been written down or recorded but have been passed from one generation to the next. Every village has its own variations. "It's like taking your mom's recipe and changing it." The dances her group does are a blend of various regional dances.

There are major differences between the continental and Azorean dances, but there are also threads of similarity, Elaine said. The mainland dances are more influenced by royalty and include minuet-style steps, so-called noble dances, as well as religious dances. Among the dances Rancho Folclórico does are the *vira*, which is like a fast waltz that comes from northern Portugal; the *chula*, a called dance also from the north; and the fast-paced *corridinho* from the south. Normally all of the dances except the *corridinho* are accompanied by singing. In parts of northern Portugal, the women sing in a high-pitched voice that is almost painful to hear.

In Portugal, the dancers perform with a larger group on stage, including a band, singers, and sometimes actors depicting aspects of village life, such as weaving, selling chickens, or herding sheep. When they can't get a live band, the American folkloric groups perform to recorded music.

One can distinguish dances from the north or south of Portugal because in the northern dances, the arms are held higher and the feet move more slowly. Also, because the weather is hotter in the south, the costumes are lighter and duller in color. Rancho Folclórico members, who make their own costumes, wear an adaptation of the northern costume, with red and black skirts or pants, vests, blouses, and aprons. The women wear scarves and the men wear hats.

Some of the folkloric groups are very serious, Linda said, but her group dances for pleasure. "We go out to have fun." If a couple can't attend a performance, the others simply form a tighter circle. If someone makes a mistake, they just dance on.

TRADITIONAL PORTUGUESE FOOD is not the best fare for a diet, but you'll never go hungry at a Portuguese woman's table. The food is plentiful, and the servings are generous.

Even in families where the rest of the diet is strictly American, a few Portuguese traditions remain. My aunt and uncle serve *linguiça* and Portuguese beans every Christmas Eve. My mother prepares dozens of different kinds of cookies, and every family gets a box. Portuguese sweet bread, with hard-boiled eggs baked in, is part of every Easter celebration.

Portuguese American mothers have passed their recipes down to their daughters. In many cases, recipes were never written down until recently. When Deolinda Avila decided to compile an Azorean cookbook, she spent many hours on intercontinental telephone calls asking her relatives to tell her how they made her favorite dishes.

The book was inspired by the Holy Spirit, Deolinda believes. Once, she wanted to bake a particular kind of Portuguese bread for the Holy Ghost celebration. Her mother-in-law had shown her how to do it before, but she ran into trouble. It was 7:30 a.m., too early to call anyone to ask questions, and there was no place to look it up. Realizing others might be having the same problem, she started putting together recipes. The result was her book, *Food of the Azores Islands.*

She did not know how to cook when she got married, Deolinda said. Every time she wanted to prepare a Portuguese dish, she would call her mother or her mother-in-law, then write down what they told her to do. "Of course, they'd just open their palm and say 'just a little bit of this or just a little bit of that.'" For her book, she measured out the ingredients, as close as she could get. "Portuguese cooking, it doesn't have to be the exact amount of the spices. No one comes out with the exact recipe. It won't taste the same, but it's still good."

In the days before microwave ovens and ready-made food, women spent most of their days in the kitchen. At one holiday dinner, Dorothy Benson and her mother noticed that Grandma had worn a path between the stove and the table. "She made the best beans I've ever tasted," Dorothy said. Her grandmother used large speckled beans with onion, garlic, cumin, and hog lard.

Louise Pitta Polsky grew up eating a blend of Madeiran and Italian food. Years later when she traveled to Madeira, she was surprised to find her cousins there eating the same foods she ate at home and growing the same vegetables—chayote, string beans, and potatoes—in their gardens.

For many Portuguese immigrant women, cooking was their claim to fame. In some cases, it was their source of income, as they got jobs on dairies or ranches cooking for large numbers of hungry men. When the family owned the ranch, the wives cooked not only for their families but for all the hired hands, too.

Living on farms, the early immigrants had a ready source of food. Eleanor Azevedo Garrissere said her father liked to fish and ate a lot of what he caught, but mostly they ate what they grew on the farm. They didn't have to stand in bread lines during the Depression. They always had *linguiça*, smoked and stored in lard.

The object was to eat, not to worry about fat or calories. Edna Sousa's uncle was a fisherman in San Diego. He used to send them huge boxes of salted fish. Every Friday, they would cut out some fish, soak it, cook it, and eat it, either by itself or in fish soup. Edna loved it.

"Talk about cholesterol city," protested her sister Virginia Silveira, who was a skinny kid partially because she couldn't stand Portuguese food. "They cooked everything to death. Vegetables were cooked until they were limp. Meat was cooked until it fell apart."

Edna said they baked their own bread. At Easter, they made sweet bread. On Ash Wednesday, they used the same dough, patted out like pancakes, cooked in oil. Virginia had a different memory: "The second day, that lard would congeal. I just couldn't eat that stuff."

Most Americans are familiar with *linguiça*, the Portuguese sausage. Once the product of all-day *festas* called *matanças*, where everyone gathered to kill the pigs and make the sausages, *linguiça* has now made it to many American grocery stores.

In Santa Clara, the place to go for *linguiça* is Neto Sausage Company on the Alameda. A family business for three generations, Neto makes the best sausage, some say. Others vote for Silva's sausage in San Jose.

Neto goes beyond *linguiça*, with a variety of foods imported from Portugal: cheese from São Jorge, frozen sardines, octopus, and cod. Their *linguiça* is fashioned in several varieties to please their customers. Portuguese old-timers like theirs with big pieces of meat and fat. Americans prefer it more finely ground and with less fat. Neto also makes Mexican chorizo sausage and *torresmos*, a marinated pork sausage.

For those who still make their own sausage, Neto sells meat, casings, and spices. "When they run out of their product, then they come and buy the *linguiça* until they make it again, but they always like to make it for themselves." Everyone has a little different idea of what they want to put in it, Bea Costa said.

Bea's family maintains the traditions, especially on the holidays. "All our children and grandchildren are used to this, which is good. I think tradition's important. People have the habit of forgetting. Their parents die, and they don't remember how they did it. My girls, they learned how to cook the Portuguese way, too."

Edith Walter said her family ate beans three times a day. She remembers a time in first or second grade when her teacher asked all the kids what they had for breakfast. She told them *feijão* and *tresums*. "I got real embarrassed because I knew I had said something that they didn't understand, but I couldn't translate it." When she got home, she asked her brother how to say it, and he told her, "Silly, that's beans and pork." "Then another time, I said I had beans and pork, and that was even worse because then they knew what it was!"

Edith said they would buy sacks of beans, potatoes, and yams and make *linguiça* and *torresmos*. They canned fruit, tomatoes, and everything else, making their own tomato sauce in big black kettles in the backyard. Her mother-in-law, Rita Lewis, canned and made jelly until the year she died. But Edith's mother gave up canning once she moved to town. "It doesn't pay," she would scold Edith, who still makes jelly, applesauce, and pickles.

The other tradition Edith upholds is cooking large quantities of food. In the old days, the grandmas always expected somebody was coming over. "When I cooked, even when I was widowed, it was hard for me to cook for one. To this day, I have platters."

When she goes to other people's homes, she gets just a salad or something small. "They come to our house, and I put platters on the table, and they say, 'How many people were you expecting?'" Friends always urge her not to make too much. When her daughters were in college, they often brought friends home. "I wouldn't just cook a pork chop or three pork chops. When my daughter Carolyn came over the other day, I fixed six pork chops. I don't just make a little pot of chicken soup; I make a pot like that." She held out her arms.

Maree Schlenker grew up eating Portuguese food. "I thought the whole world was Portuguese. I didn't realize." Her grandmother always had a big pot of soup going. In her garden, she grew kale, onions, and other ingredients. "She always cooked so if a family of ten came by, we would have enough."

Fat was not a concern. They would butcher a pig every year to make *linguiça*, *morcela*, *torresmos*, and other pork dishes. Maree's husband, Ken, was appalled when he first had *linguiça* and saw the big globs of fat in it.

Maree's grandmother liked to pick wild mushrooms. Lacking a more scientific test, she always tossed a silver coin in the pot. If it stayed silver, the mushrooms were safe to eat. Several other Portuguese women mentioned this same test, although their descendants wondered if they were just lucky not to eat any poisonous ones.

Mary Alves was known for her *vinha d'alhos*, a wine and garlic sauce in which she marinated pork. She taught her daughter-in-law Kay Alves how to make it, and Kay carries on the tradition, cooking forty pounds of pork every Christmas. The only way to learn was to watch because Mary would use "a handful of this and a glug-glug of that," she said.

The traditional style of eating was not always the healthiest. Richard Alves remembered his dad loved French bread and milk with sugar and could make a meal of it three times a day. His mother loved salt, which may be why she suffered from high blood pressure. In those days, no one knew the dangers.

As the years pass, only the favorite Portuguese dishes remain on some menus. "We still eat the Portuguese foods," Mary Machado said. "But there's certain foods that I like that are from the old tradition that my kids are not too much for. My husband used to love soups, my turnip soups, kale soups, oh we were raised with it. My son hates it, my youngest daughter hates it. My son used to say, 'Ma, when I get married, in my house, no kale, no turnips.'"

Eva Gomes has always cooked Portuguese-style. Her daughter, Donna, loved her soup. "It tasted so good and always smelled good." Now Donna's Irish-English husband, Scot, has the recipes and cooks Portuguese food. At Christmas he fixes *bacalhau*, Portuguese beans, and *vinha d'alhos*. They buy sweet bread from Souza's bakery in Santa Clara and cook fava beans picked off the bush in their front yard. Eva said that because she is diabetic, she can't eat many of her favorite foods now, but Donna said her mother's cooking still has a Portuguese flavor.

Sylvia Carroll said her mother and her aunt made sweet bread, *linguiça*, and *vinha d'alhos*. They prepared sweet rice pudding but never served rice as a side dish. So when Sylvia went away to college, she was surprised to find the rice served there wasn't sweet.

Mary Cabral O'Reilly said she makes Portuguese soup and sweet bread, but her husband is not Portuguese, so she doesn't cook many of the old-country foods. "Besides, who wants to eat sardines out of a can like my mother and father did?"

Donna Gomes Austin discovered on her trip to the Azores that she didn't like a steady diet of Portuguese food. "By the end of the fifth day, I just wanted an omelet."

But when Donna was a young nun at the Notre Dame convent, she realized how much a part of her life Portuguese food was. "We always had corned beef and cabbage, every week. We had all these

Englishy things, and I really missed the *linguiça* and the sweet bread and all that." Her dad, who sold *linguiça*, dried cod, yams, and other Portuguese food at his market in Santa Clara, brought five pounds of *linguiça* to the convent one day. It was enough to feed all sixty-five nuns there.

"The cook had to go in the basement to cook it because she didn't want to smell up everything. That's when I really felt Portuguese because I thought, how odd, that's the best smell. I missed that smell. I felt so homesick all the time." When the cooks brought out the *linguiça* and sweet bread for dinner, the nuns gave it a cool reception. "They all went, 'Eew, what is this stuff?' That's when I knew I was really different."

Reflecting on everyday meals in Portuguese homes, Donna Gomes Austin responded eloquently: "I guess if I had one word for my grandmother's cooking, it would be *sopas*. My grandmother always had a pot of soup on the stove simmering. In that pot, there was always some onions and garlic, some type of meat or bone, kale, and maybe a rice or noodle or bean added. The variety and flavors were hot and tasty. She served cornmeal with favas and kale in it. Sometimes she just cut squares of cornmeal and let us eat it cold. Sometimes she fried it in butter.

"If I had one word for my mother's cooking, it would be vegetables! Salads, carrots, spinach, broccoli, cauliflower—raw and cooked. Cucumbers marinated in vinegar or lemon juice, and spices. Carrot and celery juice, sliced tomatoes and cottage cheese. Salmon stew over rice, *açorda* (we pronounced it *assootha*), which was onions, garlic, tomato paste, and broth, with eggs dropped into it. We had lots of fish, too. My mother made a great egg sandwich with finely chopped onion loaded in the egg mixture, fried and served on bread. I think our food was basically well-balanced and nutritious. *Linguiça*, pancakes, or eggs was a Sunday brunch thing. *Vinha d'alhos* was a very-special-occasion food, like for Christmas and Easter. A day would not go by without an onion or garlic used. Those were the days, when I didn't have to cook! How I miss those days!"

Woman preparing traditional sopas *for a festa in Vila Nova, Portugal, 1975*

These days, Portuguese American women don't always have time to cook the traditional dishes. Like other women who spend more time at work than at home, Goretti Silveira said she doesn't cook much Portuguese food. "I keep saying I've got to learn." But she enjoys eating *bacalhau* and kale soup at her mother's house.

Mary Giglitto said, "I don't cook. I admit it." But that doesn't mean she doesn't eat Portuguese food. Her mother taught her husband how to make the dishes she remembers from the Azores, and he does most of the cooking at their house.

Even modern immigrants long for the familiar food from home. Nazaria Soares had a hard time when she arrived in the United States as a teenager. Her first Big Mac nearly made her sick. She couldn't bear the smells of catsup and mayonnaise. She was not used to canned food and was accustomed to only fresh beef, chicken, or pork. She didn't like her first pizza, either. Today, she serves a blend of Portuguese, Mexican (from her husband), and American foods, combining the best of all three cultures.

If today's Portuguese Americans don't cook traditional fare at home, they can still satisfy a craving for *bacalhau* or *sopas* at *festas* and other community events, as well as at Portuguese restaurants. A Portuguese feast may include *caldo verde*, a hearty green soup made with sausage, kale, and potatoes; *arroz de galinha*, fricasseed chicken with rice; a simple green salad with green-pepper rings and sliced onions; *arroz doce*, rice pudding cooked with cinnamon and egg yolks; or Portuguese sweet bread. Other popular dishes include *cozido à portuguesa*, a combination of pork cuts, *linguiça*, vegetables, and chicken boiled together in one pot; *sopas e carne*, a thick meat soup; *feijão com linguiça*, beans and sausage; *morcela frita*, fried blood sausage; and *bacalhau à Beira Alta*, baked salt cod in tomato sauce with potatoes and hard-cooked eggs. *Suspiros*, airy meringue cookies, or *filhoses*, fried donuts, are also popular.

A typical restaurant meal generally features fish or pork, served with both rice and fried potatoes, as well as hard rolls, salad, and a sweet flan or rice pudding for dessert. Wine is essential. In Portugal, every meal except breakfast is accompanied by wine, either the rich red ports and burgundies or the popular *vinhos verdes*. Literally meaning green wines, *vinhos verdes* can actually be either red or white, but are called green because they're consumed young, usually within a year after harvest.

THE TYPICAL Portuguese girl grows up stitching. My great-grandmother, grandmother, and aunts all crocheted, embroidered, and sewed. My mother added needlepoint and knitting to her repertoire. Her chair in the living room is devoted to crafts. There is always a pattern on the table beside her and a needlepointed bag containing works in progress. Her needlework is her art. On Thursday afternoons, she joins her *comadres* (friends), some Portuguese and some not, for several hours of stitchery and gossip at the senior center that occupies my former elementary school. One day not long ago, I joined them with my own embroidery.

Mom remembers that her Grandma Anna Souza spent her days with the four C's: cooking, cleaning, canning, and crocheting. "She always had a crochet hook in her hand." She couldn't afford to buy gifts, so she made things. She did fine filet crochet work on lacy collars, doilies, tablecloths, and bedspreads.

Aunt Nellie McKee, who cared for her mother in her later years, filled her own house with handmade things. She could look at an afghan or doily and determine how to make it without ever seeing a written pattern.

Kay Alves said her mother-in-law, Mary Alves, always had a basket of needlework by her chair, usually filled with crocheting or tatting. In addition to making doilies and table scarfs, she crocheted spreads for all three beds in her house. She only stopped when arthritis crippled her in her later years.

"Wherever you travel in Portugal, you see sheep grazing and hear needles clicking," says a 1987 *Family Circle* article. Portuguese Americans have continued the tradition here, passing their expertise down to their daughters and granddaughters.

Delia Mendes displaying her crochet work, 1997

I grew up the same way, learning to embroider very young. I made clothes for my dolls and stashed tablecloths, pillowcases, dish towels, and bureau scarves in a cedar chest for my future married life. I was surprised to discover most American girls didn't do this.

Back in the old country, needlework was part of a girl's required curriculum. Deolinda Avila recalled, "My mother kept me busy all the time. I had embroidery classes. I couldn't sit home just playing. I used to go three days a week to embroidery classes."

Mary Giglitto's mother also insisted she learn embroidery. She couldn't go out to play until she had done her daily stitching. Some days, she ran next door to her aunt's house, and her loving *tia* did her embroidery while Mary played. Mary has a set of embroidered towels she refuses to use because she remembers the agony that went into making them.

For Marie Gambrel, sewing was a necessity and a source of income. She made clothes for everyone in the family and also sewed for the neighbors for extra money. Everything she entered in the county fair won blue ribbons. Now the old sewing machine that used to sit in the living room rests in her mobile home, more decorative than useful. She sewed so much she got tired of it, she admitted. As a young woman, she used to embroider dish towels and pillow cases with cross-stitch and lazy daisy stitches, but after she married she didn't have time anymore.

Josephine Silva includes pictures of her fabric art on her web site on the Internet. She has a degree in apparel design and paints in watercolor, but her favorite medium is cloth, whether she makes clothing, stuffed animals, or pillows. "I spend all my life making things beautiful," she said. She believes the creativity comes from her Portuguese roots. Her mother did not sew, but Josephine's Portuguese grandmother made all of her clothing by hand. She also did tatting and lace, and Josephine was in awe of her handiwork. Josephine crochets and does other needlework, although sewing is her favorite. "I just sew all the time. It just comes out of me."

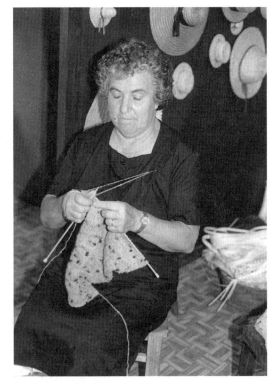

Woman knitting in Pico, 1990

When Josephine visited the artisan school in Pico, she was fascinated. "I would have given an arm and a leg to study there," she said. In fact, she asked how she could enroll and was told only Azorean residents are admitted.

One of those Azoreans who works at the artisan school in Santo Amaro, Pico, is Delia Mendes's sister. Delia, herself a master of filet crochet, modestly claims her sister is much more talented than she is. She shows off some of the flowers she has made out of fish scales, a popular art in Pico. At the artisan school, the women crochet, knit, and weave. They spin their own yarn. Her sister said the ladies get sleepy working on their crafts all day while tourists watch. They fall asleep, wake up, drink a little espresso, then go back to work.

When asked where she learned to crochet, Delia, who left the Azores at age nineteen, said, "Everybody learns it there—when we're two and three years old. We were very poor, we didn't have needle and thread. As soon as we can get some, we see the older people crocheting so we start."

She works with fine white or beige thread, creating intricate patterns on tablecloths, doilies, and bedspreads. She spreads out a Portuguese pattern, like a grid, with the instructions in Portuguese. Sometimes she makes things with no pattern, trusting her memory of what she has seen. She displayed a tablecloth like one she saw in Portugal. "When I come back, I make one." She orders threads and patterns from Portugal or from Casanova Imports in San Jose. You can't get the same materials in Sacramento, she said. "They don't have nothing Portuguese in Sacramento. No thread, food, everybody bakes their own bread."

Crochet is Delia's art and her therapy after long days working in a school cafeteria. "I love to do this. I just do it when I watch TV, when I can't sleep."

Not all Portuguese American women have succumbed to the lure of needle and thread or yarn. Pauline Correia Stonehill said her mother taught her to embroider, but she doesn't do it anymore. "I decided that was not my calling in life." She prefers ceramics, and several of her creations decorate her living room.

Donna Gomes Austin also failed to inherit the needlework gene. Her aunt Lydia had closets full of crocheted things, and her mother, Eva Gomes, was a topnotch seamstress who made her daughters' dresses, including Donna's prom dress. When Donna's mother tried to teach her to sew, she got her fingers caught in the machine. Later at the convent, the nuns also tried. "I was the only one who went backward. My hands would get all sweaty."

Others began doing needlework later in life. The late Germana Silvera Sarmento made most of her family's clothing, but she didn't learn to crochet until she was in her nineties. She reportedly made seventy-five afghans for her family and friends although her eyesight was failing. "She did it mostly by feel," her daughter Marian Janovich said in Germana's *San Jose Mercury News* obituary.

In the Azores, women are still doing the same crafts, many selling them on street corners. A woman stopped me on the street in São Miguel to show me her crocheted tablecloths. At the artisan school in Pico, we watched women spinning yarn and knitting sweaters, and at a community dinner in Faial, the women lined up at tables, selling dolls, table runners, pillows, afghans, and other crafts. They reminded me of my mother and her friends. I brought dolls made of yarn and straw and a crocheted table runner home to my mother to show how her *comadres* in Faial—who could be distant cousins—are doing the same things she does at her senior center and at home in her chair by the window.

11

Descendants Keep Stories Alive

 WHEN KATHERINE VAZ started writing about the Portuguese, the words flowed easily, as if they had been waiting for her to call them out. Katherine, whose father grew up on the Azorean island of Terceira, had been writing fiction since she was twelve years old but never expected to be billed as the first Portuguese American to publish a novel about the Portuguese in the United States. Her three books, *Saudade, Fado and Other Stories*, and *Mariana*, have brought her acclaim and avid readers.

"When I started writing about my own background as I know it and about my father's family, the words just seemed to come in a way that made me happy, so I just kept on doing it."

Alfred Lewis was actually the first Portuguese American to publish a novel in the United States, Katherine said. His book, *My Home is an Island*, came out in 1951, but hers is the first contemporary Portuguese American novel released by a major New York publisher (St. Martin's Press).

Katherine is an associate professor of English at UC Davis, a position she was glad to take so she could be close to her family after spending several years in Southern California. She only fell into full-time teaching recently, she said, but she has always wanted to write. "It took me a long time to find my stride. It was always something I wanted to do, and it seemed like something I was going to do. What the world was going to do with it remained to be seen. I feel most alive when I'm writing stories."

Saudade, published in 1994, is a mystical story of an Azorean girl, Clara, who is born mute and speaks in a language of sugar crystals. Her world is one where ghosts appear regularly, and the unexpected is ordinary. When her parents both die, she is left in the hands of a priest who is supposed to care for her and take her to claim a parcel of land she has inherited in California. Instead he endeavors to cheat her out of her property. Clara triumphs over the priest, finds love with a kind widower, and learns to communicate in a marvelous language of colors, translating numbers, words, and even musical notes into colors.

Much of *Saudade* takes place in the central valley town of Lodi. Katherine grew up in Castro Valley, but she always liked Lodi, where her godmother lived. Although the book is fiction, part of it comes from real life. Her godmother's housekeeper, like Clara, could not comprehend words and numbers. Katherine's father, a history teacher and a painter, devised a color code for her.

Saudade has been compared to *Like Water for Chocolate* and other Latin American works filled with supernatural happenings. Katherine, who teaches a course in magical realism in world literature, said the magic in her writing comes from her Portuguese culture. The color-coded language is one of her favorite parts. "I thought, what a wonderful metaphor that is, but it's a real one. I think of magic as quite a sensible view of the world rather than just the imagination running wild."

The title *Saudade* expresses a mixture of homesickness, nostalgia, longing, and sadness. In a 1995 *Bookcase* magazine interview, Katherine described it as follows: "There is this feeling that your children are going to grow up and leave you. So that affects just about everything in the way you deal with them. It happens in a lot of cultures, but the Portuguese have applied this word to it. [*Saudade*] is very un-American because Americans feel that you can take your fate and shape it a certain way, and things can be better. The Portuguese are much more fatalistic than Americans. And so *saudade* would apply to a culture that is much more fatalistic because you don't have a sense of being able to manipulate your own destiny."

Saudade was warmly received by both critics and readers. Barnes & Noble included the book in its Discover Great New Writers series. The novel was scheduled to be published in Portuguese in 1998 and has been included in American Literature courses at the University of the Azores.

Vaz's short story collection, *Fado and Other Stories*, published in 1997 by the University of Pittsburg Press, won the Drue Heinz Literature Prize. Her stories have been published in more than a dozen literary magazines. She has also published nonfiction, including book reviews for the *Boston Globe* and a piece on *fado* singing for the *New York Times*.

Katherine's latest book, *Mariana*, was first published in Europe; by late 1997, it had been sold in six languages and more than 100 countries. The novel is based on the life of a seventeenth century Portuguese nun, Mariana Alforcado, who fell in love with a French colonel during the Portuguese war for independence from Spain. Katherine originally planned to do a new translation of the love letters the real Mariana wrote during her love affair. As she searched through the Portuguese records and Mariana's writings, Katherine was so enchanted by the saga that she decided to write it as a novel. "That was the way it spoke to me," she explained.

Katherine had visited the Azores with her family. To research *Mariana*, she traveled to mainland Portugal more than a dozen times. The curator of the museum in Mariana's home town of Beja opened his extensive collection of books about the nun to Katherine and showed her Mariana's estate. "I kind of breathed it all in," she said.

As a result of her writing, Katherine has been asked to speak at numerous events in the United States and Portugal. She was selected as a member of the Luso-American contingent to welcome the Portuguese prime minister when he came to Washington D.C. in 1997. She belongs to the Luso-American Education Foundation and the Portuguese Historical and Cultural Society. "You try to go to a few things," she said.

Katherine grew up knowing the Portuguese culture. Although her Irish American mother was not Portuguese, she learned the language and encouraged the family to speak Portuguese at home, to attend the local *festas*, and to treasure their Azorean heritage. Katherine credits her with her writing gifts. "I got all the material from my father's side of my family, but the love of telling stories came from my mother's."

When people today describe her as a Portuguese writer, she is flattered. To be received so warmly by her own people feels good. Often when she gives talks, members of the audience come up afterward with tears in their eyes, saying a character she has described sounds just like their grandmother or someone else in their family.

MUCH OF AMERICAN history has been captured in the writings of the early settlers. Diaries, letters, and articles tell what it was like in the early days. But the first generations of Portuguese immigrants left no written record. Unschooled and frequently illiterate, they could only tell their stories aloud and hope their children remembered.

Today's Portuguese American women are determined to preserve as many of their families' stories as they can by writing them down. Many are researching their families' genealogical records, compiling family trees, and piecing together the stories of their immigrant ancestors. They have gathered family photos into books to pass on to their children. Several have gone a step further, writing and publishing books at their own expense, so that their descendants will have a record of their Portuguese families. These books may never show up at the major national bookstore chains but are circulated through families, Portuguese cultural organizations and publications, and most recently on the Internet.

Members of the Portuguese Historical and Cultural Society prowled the Pocket, Newcastle, and other heavily Portuguese neighborhoods in Sacramento to compile an encyclopedic record of the families that settled there. Their book, *Portuguese Pioneers of the Sacramento Area*, sold out quickly after it was published in 1990.

Mary Simas was another writer who wanted to capture her family history. Although her writings were never published in a book, she left numerous articles that are now stored in the archives at the San Jose Historical Museum. "Reflections Within My Kaleidoscope" offers memories of Mary's Portuguese American childhood, including stories of her grandparents' and parents' trips to America, her father's efforts to help build Five Wounds Church, the 1919 flu epidemic, and Mary's life on a ranch in Santa Clara. Another article, "The Portuguese Dairymen of Lawrence Road," documents life in the days before dairies and orchards gave way to high technology firms. Her notes on SPRSI give an overview of one of the largest Portuguese women's lodges. Each article adds another piece to the history of Portuguese immigrants in Santa Clara Valley.

Many other Portuguese writers have tried to put their memories and their feelings on paper for the next generation. Geraldine Souza La Shell of Auburn told the story of her parents' immigration to Nevada and eventually to California in a 1,200-verse poem called "Mom and Dad," which is available at the Auburn-Placer County Library. Adrienne Serpa Alston of Tulare paid tribute to her ancestors in a booklet she titled *Beloved Emigrants—A Journey of the Heart*. Florence Ineas Nunes of Rancho Cordova published a book of poetry, *Songs of Saudade*. Mari Lyn Salvador wrote *Festas Açoreanas: Portuguese Religious Celebrations in California and the Azores*, which was published by the Oakland Museum history department.

Male writers have also shared their memories. Robert L. Santos of Denair published the nonfiction book *Azoreans to California: A History of Migration and Settlement* and the novel *Flight of the Hawk*

Islanders: An Azorean Emigrant Story. Art Coelho of Montana is a one-man publishing industry, writing and producing many poems and stories, complete with illustrations of his family life when he was growing up in the San Joaquin Valley. His exhibit, "To the Azores and Back," combining his paintings and poetry, has been shown in many California cities.

The various Portuguese lodges have published commemorative books as part of their 100th anniversary celebrations. Carlos Almeida's 1978 *Portuguese Immigrants: The Centennial Story of the Portuguese Union of the State of California* not only gives a complete history of UPEC, but offers useful information on the Portuguese in both Portugal and the United States. Goretti Silveira's publishing company, Bridge Publications, published IFES's anniversary book, and SPRSI members planned to turn their memories into a book for their 1998 centennial celebration.

A seminar in the Azores on Azorean folklore inspired Cecilia Cardoza Emilio to write and self-publish *Azorean Folk Customs.* No one else seemed to offer information on such things as the old songs and dances, the Holy Ghost Festivals, courting rituals, and other things that were commonly part of Azorean life but were quickly disappearing from the lives of Portuguese in the United States. All the books she could find on the subject were written in Portuguese, a major roadblock to Portuguese Americans who could not read in that language.

The Portuguese government had invited San Diego's Portuguese Historical Center to send a representative. Cecilia, secretary of the group, was chosen to go. Although her father was born in Pico, she had never been to the islands. The three-week seminar was held in Angra, the capital of Terceira, and she had an opportunity to visit all nine islands. She loved them so much she has gone back twice since the seminar.

Cecilia, a retired Spanish teacher, had not written a book before. "I hadn't the faintest idea how to start, but I was determined to do it." She read everything she could find on Azorean folklore, working her way slowly through the books in Portuguese. Many of the books she read came from Portugal or on interlibrary loan from the J.A. Freitas Library run by the UPEC lodge in San Leandro.

It took her a year to finish the book. She paid all the printing costs herself. Word spread through the Portuguese community and various Portuguese American publications, and she quickly sold all of her 500-copy first edition. She went on to do four more printings of the book. People are grateful to find information in English about the things they have only heard alluded to by their elders—the *chamarrita*, the *matança*, the story songs, the superstitions. Why, for instance, does Grandma throw salt over her shoulder? What is the *festa* about, besides a parade and free *sopas*?

Cecilia writes in her preface: "It is in the folk customs that one can find the roots and the soul of the people; or as said in Portuguese, *No folclore achamos a raiz e alma do povo.*" In her book, she attempts to preserve those roots and make them accessible to the generations that follow.

The daughter of Portuguese immigrants, Pauline Correia Stonehill grew up on a dairy in California's Central Valley. Her mother liked to tell stories of the old days, and Pauline, blessed with a good memory, would repeat the same stories to her children. Her sons urged her to publish them, and a friend who was a printer offered to print the book. Pauline had inherited a little money from her sister-in-law and decided that publishing her family stories would be a good way to use it.

She organized her pieces in chronological order and filled in the parts that were still missing, hurrying to get the book finished in time for Christmas. *A Barrelful of Memories: Stories of My Azorean Family* was ready in December 1995. The book starts in 1891, when her mother's father was smuggled in a barrel aboard an American-bound ship. It finishes with her father's death in 1945. It was a tough life. The family faced disease, poverty, political upheaval, and the never-ending demands of running a dairy.

The book describes life in Terceira and the early years in America. Pauline's maternal grandmother, whom she called Madrinha (godmother), did laundry, picked cranberries, shucked

Doris Machado Van Scoy's book, A Quest for the Story of Antonio and Maria

corn, and cleaned houses while her husband worked on a dairy and later for the railroad. Madrinha, a midwife, delivered babies and was always on call to help the sick. At home, she did much of the cooking and housework along with Pauline's mother.

Pauline's father, Frank Correia, struggled throughout his life with chronic illness and risked his health and his farm to organize a dairymen's association. Pauline, a bright child who would eventually go to college and become a teacher, grew up surrounded by a loving family who protected her from the worst moments and left her with many sweet memories.

In her book, Pauline details the low points—such as the day when all of the family's cows were taken away in a dispute between the dairymen and local authorities over tuberculosis testing—as well as the high points, including the annual *festas*, Portuguese band concerts, her mother's beer-making efforts during Prohibition, and her uncle's secret career as a boxer.

By spring 1997, Pauline had sold approximately 500 copies of her book. Readers told her they couldn't stop reading once they started. People would thank her for telling her stories, which were much like their own Portuguese families' stories. Some of the letters were so heartfelt they made her cry, Pauline said.

Retired schoolteacher Doris Machado Van Scoy turned the story of her paternal grandparents into *A Quest for the Story of Antonio and Maria*. She went back to the site of the family home, talked to neighbors and family, researched the history of her Azorean grandparents, and wrote their story, typing it painstakingly on a typewriter and paying thousands of dollars to have 500 copies professionally printed and bound. The whole process took seventeen years.

"I am not a writer," Doris insisted. "Nor do I know about publishing and marketing and such." She had tried several regional publishers before deciding to publish her book without their help. "I'm not comfortable with selling myself," she explained.

Doris's paternal grandparents, the subjects of the book, both died when she was a child, so she never knew them well. Antonio, like many, was smuggled onto a whaling ship and jumped ship in California. He returned to Faial to find a wife, choosing fourteen-year-old Maria to wear the white dress he had brought from America. They came back to California, living in an adobe hut for years until Antonio could afford to buy land and build a real wood-frame house. As the years passed, Maria bore fifteen children, and Antonio worked the land with his sons. The book follows Antonio and Maria through an earthquake, deaths, and a devastating fire to their own deaths four months apart.

In addition to telling the story of her grandparents, Doris also describes her efforts to learn about her family's history, her struggles with the Portuguese language, and her experiences as she met people who had known her family in the early days.

Doris grew up in America, but was able to reconnect with her Portuguese roots through her writing. "This book has put me into the world of the Portuguese in California," she said.

The book sold well, but Doris said even if it didn't make any money, it was worth doing as a record for her children and grandchildren. She wished someone had left her something in writing about the old days. "If I had had one page..."

Her book, and those of other Portuguese women who write their family histories, are legacies for those who follow.

"I NEVER THOUGHT I would live to see this day," Mary Machado said, looking up at the new Portuguese Historical Museum when it opened on June 7, 1997, in San Jose.

Mary sat in an electric wheelchair, a pleated parasol protecting her face from the blazing sun. The first guests were inside the 1,600 square-foot museum, which still smelled of sawdust and fresh paint. There they saw a map of the Azores etched in glass, mannequins dressed up as *festa* queens, pictures of Portuguese celebrations, Portuguese dairies and fruit ranches, Portuguese cannery workers, Portuguese businesses, and more. Empty spaces remained where future exhibits would go as the committee gathered more money and materials.

Earlier in the day, Mary had sat with a group of friends under the trees at the San Jose Historical Museum complex watching a parade that wound all around the park. Among those marching was her son Joe, leader of the group that built the museum. He left the line to give his mother *um abraço* (a hug) and tell her, "We did it, Ma." Remembering that proud moment, Mary's eyes filled with tears. She shook her head. "I'm sorry. I get emotional when I think about it."

Mary was not alone in her happy tears that day. Approximately 3,000 Portuguese Americans, ranging from toddlers to old men and women, celebrated both the museum opening and the annual *Dia de Portugal*. The day began with the parade. Dancers performed traditional dances from the Azores, Madeira, and continental Portugal. Officials spoke of the need to preserve the Portuguese heritage and thanked those who had donated time, money, and labor to build the museum. The climax of the day came as everyone gathered around the museum entrance to watch Joe Machado lead the ribbon-cutting. Father Leonel Noia of Five Wounds Church blessed the new building, two doves were released into the air, and the people moved forward into the museum to see the special place where their memories would be saved and honored.

The museum project began back in the 1980s with a handful of people from the Cabrilho Cultural Center, of which Joe Machado was president. They joined forces with the Portuguese Chamber of

Portuguese Historical Museum, San Jose, 1997

Commerce, won approval from the city of San Jose to build it at the San Jose Historical Museum, and recruited contributions from the Portuguese community. The groups planning the museum coalesced into the Portuguese Heritage Society. Their dream was to build an *império*, a Holy Ghost chapel just like the one that used to be at Five Wounds Church.

The San Jose Historical Museum, spread out over twenty-five acres in southeast San Jose, has been laid out to resemble turn-of-the-century San Jose, with many actual old buildings moved there and others recreated to look like the originals. The Portuguese museum sits next to the Chinese Ng Shin Gung chapel and across the way from the old livery stables.

The *império* stands in a large plaza bearing a reproduction of the "Rosa dos Ventos," a compass rose made of Portuguese tile just like the one at the Monument of the Discoveries in Lisbon honoring

Portuguese explorers. Two bandstands, replicas of those that flanked the original *império*, stand on either side.

At the kickoff celebration for the museum, Joe Machado told the assembled crowd of Portuguese Americans how his parents had emigrated from the Azores and worked on farms in the Central Valley and San Jose. Their story, and those of thousands of others, would be preserved in the museum. "It is their struggle, their experience, their defeats, their victories that is our shared heritage. Our museum remembers and honors their stories. These stories must be preserved for your children and grandchildren. They will want to know and will want to remember."

City councilmember Margie Fernandes, a third-generation Portuguese American and the council liaison for the project, said, "I'm sorry to say I've lost touch with my culture, but this museum will bring it back to me, and my story will be told a thousand times to people of Portuguese descent who will come to this wonderful museum."

Edith Walter worked on the museum from the beginning. "It's about time we all get together and try to have something," she said. The Portuguese are a hidden nationality. "We sort of keep to ourselves; that's the problem. We don't advertise ourselves."

At the Chinese Ng Shin Gung temple next door, Santa Clara Valley's Chinese residents hold many activities, including a huge annual festival. The Portuguese will need to do the same to keep the money coming in, Edith noted.

The Portuguese Museum, like most construction projects, cost more than the organizers expected. The Heritage Society held dinners, picnics, radio pledge drives, and other fundraisers. The city of San Jose, the Portuguese government, and private donors all donated funds. Most of the labor was provided by volunteers using materials either donated or paid for with cash donations. It came from the same type of energy that enabled the Portuguese to build Five Wounds Church around World War I and to rebuild the IES hall next door after it burned down in the early 1990s.

Edith and other members of the society collected written material, photos, and memorabilia to put in the museum. Edith was a queen at two different *festas* and contributed photographs, along with the actual outfits her daughters wore when they marched as queen and sidemaid in the *festa* parade. Many other families raided their photo albums and cedar chests for items to display in the museum.

Edith, a docent at San Jose Historical Museum and frequent participant in museum fashion shows, discovered several years ago that most of the docents didn't know much about the Portuguese. She led them on a tour to Five Wounds Church and Sousa's restaurant in Little Portugal. She showed them a real *império* and told them about the Portuguese customs surrounding it. Since then, several volunteers have come forward saying they are also Portuguese.

One of those volunteers was interior designer Patricia Borba McDonald. A descendant of Azorean immigrants, McDonald said her work with the Portuguese Heritage Group on the museum rejuvenated her interest in the Portuguese culture. Several years before, when she was president of the San Jose Historical Museum Association, she attended a State of the City breakfast. A table reserved for the Portuguese Chamber of Commerce was occupied entirely by men. She asked these men why there was nothing at the San Jose Historical Museum about the Portuguese, who had played a big part in the city's history. The men just pointed at each other, she recalled. However, not long after, the idea surfaced to build a Portuguese museum.

McDonald volunteered her time to design the altar and display cases, choose finishes for the floors and walls, and fine-tune the lighting plans. Many other people donated a lot of time to make this museum a reality, she noted.

Mary and Ed Pasqual are on the museum board. Ed, a masterful woodworker and professional upholsterer, made the altar and display cases for the *império* from McDonald's designs. He had previously spent five years working on the renovation of St. Clare's Church, refurbishing the altar and the stations of the cross.

Festa *queens marching in the* Dia de Portugal *parade, San Jose, 1997*

At first, the emphasis was on getting the museum built. Once it became a reality, the group turned its attention to fundraising. In addition to asking for donations, they sold bricks in the museum's Wall of Honor. Each brick is engraved with a family name. The Portuguese community has money to contribute, but you have to have to show people what they're paying for, Mary Pasqual said.

Mary Simas always wanted San Jose to have a Portuguese museum. She attended the groundbreaking but didn't live to see the museum open. Her daughter, Maree Simas Schlenker, spent months commuting from her home in Roseville to San Jose for meetings to plan the museum. "My dedication is for my mother," she said.

"I think it really is going to be something great for the children of the community because so little is known about the Portuguese in a lot of areas," Maree said. She envisions symposiums, field trips for children, and *festas* at the new museum. Those who buy bricks and have their family names inscribed will be able to honor their ancestors, she added.

Sylvia Carroll fell into the museum project by accident in 1993. She had heard an announcement on a Portuguese radio station about some event at the Historical Museum. Being a docent there, she decided to attend. It turned out to be the ribbon-cutting for the Portuguese Museum. She quickly volunteered to help, becoming treasurer and publicity chair for the Heritage Society. She felt it was a shame more American families did not attend the groundbreaking and the parade that followed the next day. The only ones who knew about it were the Portuguese. "We've got to tell the other people about it," she said.

Judging by the size of the crowd that attended the opening of the museum, the word is spreading. In a society that is becoming more ethnically mixed with every generation, the museum offers a place where those of Portuguese heritage can look back and see where it all started.

12

Grandma Never Went Back

THE NAME Mary Cabral is very common among California Portuguese. But in Sacramento, the name refers to one very special woman. Mary Souza Cabral of Sacramento was eighty-seven years old when I interviewed her. We had met on a tour of Portugal in 1990. She went with her daughters, Viola and JoAnn. They had gone on the same tour before, taking side trips to visit relatives in Pico, and they have gone several times since. Sometimes, we younger folk worried about Mary on our trip. She seemed so small and fragile, but she was tough and determined. Whenever we encountered Portuguese natives, Mary would charge up and start a conversation. Within minutes, they were old friends.

Mary was no ordinary housewife, she was happy to tell you. She pointed proudly to the picture of her that was published in the Portuguese Historical and Cultural Society's book on Portuguese pioneers. She was delighted when an enlargement of that picture, taken in the days when she hosted a local radio show, was displayed at the Sacramento History Museum. Over the years, she had met many dignitaries from California and Portugal and was still collecting praises and awards for her life's work.

My husband and I went to see her one day in January, not long after Christmas. She was waiting for us, anxiously brewing chicken soup on the stove. Before we could sit down, she took us on a tour of the house, proudly showing us photos of her children, grandchildren, and great-grandchildren. Then she insisted we have some cake and soda. When we couldn't eat anymore, she brought out a case full of cassette tapes.

Mary shuffled through dozens of tapes, plucked one out, and clicked it into the recorder. We heard the song "April in Portugal," followed by Mary's voice welcoming listeners in Portuguese to the show she hosted in the 1950s on KROY. Proudly, she played one tape after another. Some were her own show, "Ecos da Capital," a mixture of music and talk. Others were a similar show, "Cartas de Portugal," recorded in the old country and sent to her as part of a cultural exchange.

Mary looked back on her seven-year radio career as the highlight of her life. She had always liked show business. She appeared in plays at St. Elizabeth's church and at Portuguese lodge conventions and boasted, "I had one week of professional theater."

Over the years, Mary made headlines as director of a Portuguese youth dance troupe. During our visit, she pulled off the shelf forty-five-year-old photos of her dancing daughters, JoAnn and Violet. She had many newspaper clippings showing her children and later her grandchildren performing Portuguese folk dances that she taught them. When I asked if she was a good dancer herself, Mary shook her head. No, but she could show other people how to do the dances.

Although she was married and had four children, Mary was more active outside the home than most Portuguese women of her generation. In addition to her lodge functions, for years she chaired the Portuguese activities at the United Nations International Dinners and at the annual Camellia Festival. Mary was thrilled in 1991 to receive a Medal of Merit of the Portuguese Communities from the

Portuguese government for her contributions to Portuguese cultural activities in California.

In her younger, pre-show business days, Mary was a traveling pear packer for the A.B. Humphrey Ranch, working wherever the company would send her. "I got so I could pack over a hundred boxes a day. That was good."

Mary was four years old when she came with her mother from Pico to this country in 1907 to join her father. She met Joe Cabral at a ranch where her mother worked as a cook. Mary was not quite fourteen years old when they were married. "I was one of those young brides," she admitted. "My mother thought he was a real good person, so that helped."

Mary and Joe had four kids, JoAnn, Violet, Betty, and Bill. Betty died in her thirties. Mary guessed she had twelve grandchildren and spoke proudly of a grandson who worked at a television station in San Diego.

For years, Joe and Mary operated a forty-acre ranch, where they grew olives and wine grapes. Later he worked as a building contractor. Joe passed away in 1983, and Mary spent her later years living alone with an energetic little white dog named Cooky. Violet lived in the house behind her, and JoAnn lived next door. Joe built all three houses on land that used to be part of the ranch.

Several years after we talked, Mary moved in with Violet. When Mary was growing up, she said, her house was always full of people. Her mother welcomed newcomers from the Azores, giving them shoes and clothes and offering a place to stay until they could get settled. Now her house was kind-of quiet.

The last time I saw Mary Cabral, she read a poem as part of a program on Portuguese women's art, literature, and music. When I saw her name on the program, I wondered if she would be nervous or have trouble reading the words. I guess I didn't know her well enough. She could barely see over the microphone, but Mary was the star of the show with her reading of "Tempo Passado."

"She's crying," whispered a woman sitting near me. Sure enough, there were tears in Mary's eyes. Her voice shook a little as she came to the emotional conclusion, but her daughter Violet just laughed when I mentioned it later.

"She's an actress, didn't you know? She can turn it on just like that."

Mary proudly posed for a photo with the Portuguese consul after the reading. Then she stood next to a large painting by Maxine Olson called "Portuguese Ladies." It showed two overweight women sitting in a hall gossiping. "I fit right in," said tiny Mary Cabral with a chuckle.

AT THE FIRST SIGHT of Terceira after our ten-hour flight from Los Angeles, my eyes filled with tears. Below me stretched an island greener than any place I'd ever seen in California. As we descended, the rock walls neatly dividing the fields into little squares became clear. Then I saw the white houses with their red tile roofs and the harbor at Angra with its rugged black coastline against the sapphire blue water. Paradise!

How lucky I was. An elderly woman who started her journey with us in San Francisco would never see what I was seeing out the window as our plane landed. She had planned a surprise visit to her family on Terceira, but the surprise turned out differently from the happy reunion she had envisioned. One hour and forty minutes before we landed, she had an asthma attack and stopped breathing. She died, stretched out across the seats of the airplane. Flight attendants desperately tried to revive her with CPR while her weeping husband looked on. When our plane landed at Lajes Airport on Terceira, there was no hurry to carry the poor woman to the waiting ambulance. It was already too late. That weekend, her funeral was held in the church in her village, and she was buried in the cemetery nearby. At least she made it home, we told each other sadly, thinking about our grandmothers who never had that opportunity.

Most of our ancestors never went back to Portugal. When they left for America, they said goodbye forever. There were no airplanes, and the journey took several grueling weeks or months on crowded boats. The early immigrants suffered through seasickness, hunger, filthy conditions, and tremendous fear of what lay ahead. What if America wouldn't let them in? What if they couldn't find anyone they knew there? What if it was worse than the land they left behind?

Even if they were willing to face the arduous journey again, few could afford it. The door to the past was closed, no matter how homesick they felt. Most families couldn't spare the money for a trip back across the Atlantic. They needed everything they earned to feed their large and growing families. Besides, they were too busy. Factory workers didn't dare ask for time off, for fear of losing their jobs. Nor could families running farms or dairies go away. Who would take care of the crops? Who would milk the cows every morning and afternoon?

Bea Costa's mother never returned to Portugal. She didn't have enough money to take the whole family and refused to leave her children with anyone else. "She never did go back again to see her mother and dad. They died without her ever going back, without ever knowing my father."

Marie Gambrel's father didn't make it back to Faial. "He never did get to go back to see his parents. The saddest thing for me when Daddy died was that he worked all his life and never got to go back to his native land. Not even once since he was nineteen years old."

The letters used to fly back and forth between California and the Azores, Maree Simas Schlenker said. Her father talked about Portugal all the time. His younger brother and sister had trouble getting into the United States after immigration restrictions were tightened. If someone was going to the old country, Maree's dad would fill a big trunk for his family with clothing and supplies, as well as money.

By the time Maree visited the Azores in 1951, her father's parents had died, so she never got to meet them. His brother and sister were admitted to the United States after President John F. Kennedy eased the restrictions in the 1960s. Maree's father had to post a $10,000 bond promising to be responsible for them.

Maree was surprised by the poverty she saw in the Azores. In the house where she stayed, the kitchen had no running water or stove. The family stored well water in a concrete container and cooked over a brick oven with a grate. They slept on straw mattresses that were flat in the mornings even though they fluffed them up every night. They had electricity for only three hours a day, 8 to 11 p.m., and the bathroom was an outhouse on the porch. Despite the rustic conditions, Maree said, "Everything was so clean and tidy. It might not have been much, but everybody took pride in their places." Things have improved since 1951, but Maree no longer flies and doesn't expect to return.

In the early days, there were no transatlantic telephone lines. Even when phone service became available, it was too costly for most immigrant families. Letters were the only connections with relatives back home. But the mail took weeks to arrive, and many of the immigrants couldn't read or write. They had to ask someone else to write their letters for them and to read the ones that came back. It wasn't a very satisfying way to communicate.

Usually, only the older relatives remained in Portugal. The younger brothers, sisters, and cousins either came together or waited for the first arrivals to send for them as soon as they earned enough money. As their American families grew, the older ones back home died, and there was no longer any reason to return. Besides, what was back there but poverty and hard work anyway? Many Portuguese immigrants never had any desire to go back.

Since World War II, it has become a lot easier to visit Portugal. While flying is expensive, many families can find a way to pay for it. However, even those who can afford to go back aren't always interested.

Nellie McKee, whose parents came from Faial as young adults, could have flown to the Azores for free. Her daughter-in-law, who worked for a major airline, had offered many times to arrange her flight, but Nellie shrugged and said, "What for? I don't know anybody there. Maybe we'll go to Epcot Center in Florida instead."

Women socializing in Lisbon, Portugal, 1990

Others spent years dreaming of going back. Mary Machado first returned to the Azores fifty years after she had left. By then, the seven-year-old girl who had left in 1915 was a widow with grown children, and her heart was firmly planted in California. Although she has since traveled to Portugal several more times, she emphasized that she only went to visit. "That's where my roots are, but I would never go to stay. I just couldn't get used to it. I was raised here," she said.

The trips can be emotional ones. Mary recalled visiting the islands with her aunt and walking from the house where she was born to the church where she was baptized. "We were going down the road, hand in hand. I looked at my aunt, and she was crying. I said, 'What happened? Why are you crying?'

"She said, 'I never thought I would live fifty years to take your hand and walk the same road to the same church where you were baptized.' That's why she was crying. Then she got me crying, and both of us were going down the road sniffling. I had a frog in my throat the rest of the day because of the way she said it. It was very touching."

THE SAYING "you can't go home again" is true for most Portuguese immigrants. Not only have the immigrants adopted American ways, but their former countrymen see them as rich Americans. Most are not rich, but they seem so in comparison. It is not unusual for California Portuguese to take suitcases full of clothing and gifts when they go back to visit. The longer they live in California, the more pronounced the differences seem.

Fatima Lopes, who emigrated in 1969, misses her friends in the Azores but said, "When I go back to Portugal, I feel foreign in my own country." In the Azores, everyone is the same, all Portuguese. In California, she mixes with Filipinos, African Americans, Mexicans, and Asians, as well as people from other parts of Portugal. "I have more friends here than I used to have in my own country."

Deolinda Avila, who came to the United States when she was fifteen, goes back often, spending vacations on Pico, where her in-laws have a summer home. While she enjoys her visits, she said, "I feel like I don't belong." Most of her old friends have emigrated, too, and things have changed in the Azores, just as they have everywhere. "You think of Portugal like it was. For a lot of people, even these Portuguese that came here and never went back, their idea of Portugal is the way it was when they came. But it isn't. It's changed. Times have changed."

Today, Deolinda said, the Portuguese are dealing with the same concerns as Americans. Young couples have to worry about day-care because Grandma isn't home to take care of the kids—she's working, too. They are having to put their aging parents in nursing homes because no one has the time to take care of them. Since the end of socialism and Portugal's entry into the European market in the 1970s, goods are more expensive, people go out to eat more, and there's more communication with the outside world. Portugal is not the same as the land the immigrants left.

For Delia Mendes, Pico isn't home anymore, although her two brothers and one sister still live there. "I go back, it's like I don't belong there anymore." She and her husband visit the Azores every few years, but are all too aware that Sacramento is their home now. Pico has gotten more modern. The young people have much more freedom than she had growing up. "It was a small village. Everything we do, everything we say, everybody knows. And now it's different." If the kids skip school in Sacramento, somebody calls their parents. In Pico, the bus takes them away to a big village, and they can go swimming all day long without their parents ever knowing.

Gui Sequeira doesn't feel at home in the Azores anymore either. She used to go back every four or five years, but hadn't gone in nine years, since she and her husband separated. She would never move back. She has lived in California longer than she lived in Pico, and it no longer feels like home, but neither does California.

As an immigrant, she missed the younger years here, Gui said. She doesn't know the nursery rhymes and traditions American kids grow up with and was not able to pass them on to her own children. "I always felt that there was a lot that they missed because I didn't know." Once they started school, her children were not interested in the old-country stories, she added.

"There's a big gap that is missing. You say you are Portuguese, and that's what your roots are, but you do not belong there. I've often thought that once you emigrate, you are a gypsy, and you do not really belong anywhere."

"You never really master the new language," Gui said, and "you lose so much of your native language. I do okay, but I always feel that I'm not in control."

Large numbers of Portuguese emigrants regularly go home to visit. Deolinda Avila said the Azoreans call these visitors the "summer flies" because they arrive with lots of money to spend and buy up all the best fish and meat, leaving second choice for the people who live there. "I'm a summer fly," Deolinda said with a sad laugh.

Goretti Silveira noted that some families do go back to Portugal to live. Although she has been in the United States since she was a teenager, she sometimes thinks about going back "to read and write and to hibernate." Now that they are retired, her parents spend four to six months a year in São Jorge, her father's home island.

In contrast, Mary Pasqual has visited the Azores but would never move back. When she visited Faial in the 1970s, the homes had no electricity, and the house she was born in had mud floors. Today, most of the homes have modern conveniences. Although she has family in Faial, she considers Santa Clara her home. "I love it here. I wouldn't leave Santa Clara." It's a big mistake for older people to move away from their homes and their friends in their later years, she said.

Whether summer flies or tourists, Portuguese Americans who visit their families' homeland still feel an emotional tug when the plane lands. "I'm in Portugal! I'm in Portugal!" Dolores Freitas Spurgeon shouted when she landed in Lisbon for the first time. She wished her parents were alive so she could tell them how she felt. "You do get a feeling of connection," said the retired college professor, who has lived her whole life in Santa Clara.

Many others have felt that connection. Al and Ginny Dutra of Mountain View first went to Portugal seeking Al's roots in the Azores. Ginny was working as a travel agent at the time, and they fell in love with the islands. There were no tours to the Azores then, so they started their own tour business. After nearly two decades, their Azorean tours are very popular, especially among Portuguese Americans.

The group of thirty-nine the Dutras took to the Azores, Madeira, and continental Portugal in 1990 was typical. More than half were of Portuguese descent. Some had plans to visit family they already knew were in Portugal. Others hoped to find relatives or evidence of their ancestors' past. For most, the trip was a success.

Dolores Silva Greenslate of Sacramento had let some of her relatives in the Azores know about the tour, and word spread that "Dolores is coming." Her cousins were waiting to shower her and her husband, Norman, with love, food, and *vinho*. Other Sacramentans also visited family. Mary Cabral and her daughters went to Pico to reconnect with relatives they had met on another trip three years earlier, and Aileen Alves Gage of Auburn visited her kin on São Jorge.

For those whose families had maintained their ties across the Atlantic, it was a rare chance to visit. For others, the trip was one of discovery. Lucy Silveira didn't think any of her family was still in the Azores, but she asked around anyway. On Terceira, she struck gold in an unexpected place. The tour bus driver, a comic little man named Manuel who knew everybody on the island, turned out to be her first cousin. The ecstatic Manuel took Lucy and her husband, Frank, home to meet his wife and kids and introduced them to everyone he met.

Sisters Wilma Barros, Mabel Goodale, and Helen Smith, three of nine siblings, also met new relatives. They had the names of cousins in São Jorge, but they didn't know exactly where they lived or what they looked like. When they asked a woman at a store in São Jorge if she knew their cousins, she turned out to be one of them.

There were many such coincidences on the trip. Bob Lewis was aware that he had kin on Faial and Pico but was surprised to find the tour guide on Faial knew his cousins. She called them, and the cousins came to meet the Lewises for dinner. Then on Pico, the cabbie who came to pick the Lewises up at the airport knew another person they were looking for and drove them straight to him.

The Azores are small. There are 260,000 people on all nine islands—less than one-third the population of San Jose. If you ask enough people, you're bound to find the families you're seeking.

American-born Sylvia Carroll has taken two trips to the Azores. In 1992, she saw advertisements for affordable trips and convinced her aunt and her cousin to go with her. On São Jorge, they asked about family members and were referred to a "Tio Alonzo," whose daughter knew Sylvia's cousin. Soon they were meeting more cousins than they ever knew they had. "So many cousins!" she exclaimed.

She went back again three years later, volunteering to help prepare for an upcoming festival. She had no idea what she was getting into. In five days, she and several other women turned 1,760 pounds of flour into loaves of bread. They beat ninety-six eggs to start—that should have been a clue. They spent all day leaning over a bowl on a stool, taking turns punching and kneading a massive pile of dough. Sylvia's muscles were so sore she could barely move.

Sylvia had made copies of her family tree to give to her relatives, but they didn't show much interest. Most had gone to fourth grade at most and were not used to reading. Until recently, there was no high school on her island, she said. Bookstores were rare in the Azores. The island of Graciosa didn't have a single one.

She found it ironic that stores in the biggest towns had bar code scanners, but down the road, the houses had no running water. On her first trip, the houses she saw used outhouses. Later they got flush toilets, but even before modern plumbing, they had electricity and television sets.

Richard and Kay Alves took the trip to the Azores that his mother never made. They met many cousins, to whom they gave pictures of his father and mother. They saw the church where his parents were married and brought home a handful of dirt from his mother's house. The house had a beautiful ocean view, but it was deserted. "When a house falls apart," Kay said, "They abandon it and build next door."

A cousin who is a priest said mass in the Alveses' honor, and cousins they had just met threw a birthday party for Kay. They were so warm and wonderful, she said.

Richard is sorry his parents never made it back. They didn't speak much of their own parents, although mail traveled back and forth. The family would hide letters inside newspapers to avoid the higher postage. "Pa always wanted to go back, but Ma said there was nothing for her," Kay said.

Some families make a habit of going back. Louise Pitta Polsky has been to Madeira three times, visiting her many cousins. The first trip was with her mother, whose parents came from Porto Santo. The second time, she went with her husband. The third trip was with her daughter, on the anniversary of her husband's death. Each time, they stayed in motels, although some of the cousins lived in the house where her father grew up. The house had no plumbing when they first visited in 1964. Although it has become more modern with each visit, Louise said there is no room for guests, so they pay for lodging in the main city of Funchal.

The first time Marie Balshor went to Portugal, she joined a church group from the Sacramento area. She had known for years that she had inherited a piece of property on the continent, and the priest with their group said he would show her where it was.

"So now we're going to look at the property. Oh my gosh. There was a pigsty and a tree—a piece of land like this to that [showing the width of her living room]. That was my inheritance. And then there was this big mound like this. And we're standing on it. Father reaches down and he picks that pebble up and says, 'Marie, I think you should take this as a remembrance of your inheritance.' The whole property was not worth more than $500."

She wrote to her cousin Maria and told her to keep that land for herself. As it turned out, the deed went back hundreds of years

Women making massa sovada *(sweet bread) for a* festa, *Vila Nova, Portugal, 1975*

and had never been changed. Transferring ownership would cost more than the land was worth.

Marie went back to Portugal with her husband, Al, in 1978, determined to put the property in her cousin's name. When they arrived, they discovered Maria had died three months earlier. Her husband had not contacted them. He had taken his daughter out of school to take care of him. The other kids were scattered. Marie never heard another word from that family.

Marie had more than one surprise waiting for her the first time she went to Portugal, where her parents and older brother had been born. Two weeks before she left, her mother-in-law, Graça Balshor, said she had something to tell her. She revealed that Al's father had had an affair before he married her. He never married the woman because she was from a different class, but they had three children together. His marriage to Graça had been arranged by their parents.

Graça, who had met her husband's illegitimate children, gave Marie money to take to Al's half-brothers in Portugal. With that mission in mind, Marie took a cab to the town of Urros, inquiring about the three brothers. Only one, Antonio, was still alive. Al's aunt and cousin arranged the introduction.

"Talk about a magic moment of life," Marie said. Her relatives took her to the shrine of Santa Plenario, the village's patron saint, for the meeting. A man rode up on a donkey. He was slender, with blue eyes and rosy cheeks. "He called me *cunhada* (sister-in-law) immediately, and I called him *cunhado*, and he invited me to his house to meet his wife and his daughter. Oh, I was so excited."

The family killed their pet chicken to eat in her honor and served her their homemade whiskey until she was "looped." She did her best to eat chicken fried in rancid oil and rice cooked in chicken blood. The house was full of people who had come to meet her.

"It was magic. And the daughter, I fell in love with her immediately." She stayed three wonderful days. When it was time for her to leave, they packed her lunch: codfish balls, fried chicken, apples and pears, goat cheese, and olives. "At six o'clock in the morning, all these people gathered to say good-bye. I felt like a queen. They all had their white handkerchiefs waving goodbye to me. They all brought me little things. I bet there was a good dozen and a half people saying goodbye to me. I saved Antonio for last. I loved him; I fell in love with this man. He held my face like this and he said, '*Cunhada, adeus.*' And he said to give love to his brothers and sisters in America, and then we hugged. I was crying so hard when I got in that cab."

Marie shook her head. "They wanted to call me Dona Maria. I got that straightened out right away. 'In America, *todos somos iguais.*' In America, we are all equal."

In 1973, Marie and Al went to Portugal for their twenty-fifth wedding anniversary, and Al got to meet his brother. It was another memorable time. "When they embraced, and they yelled 'Brother!' at each other, it was magic." Antonio, who remembered seeing his younger brother when he was a boy, wouldn't let him out of his sight, Marie said.

Before leaving on their trip, they had decided to buy a gift for Antonio. Marie found a good sale at JC Penney and bought him a suit, guessing at the size. It fit just right, and the blue in the tie matched his eyes. It needed only a little hemming, which his daughter did. Antonio was so happy he danced and sang. When Antonio died a few years later, he was buried in that suit. "I felt so good," said Marie, remembering that inexpensive but handsome brown suit. "Those are things again of life that you have to experience. Marvelous."

The first time Maria Sykora went back to Portugal, she arrived in Lisbon on the very day in 1974 that the revolution to overthrow the old government began. She laughed at her naiveté. "When I saw the tanks, I thought it was a parade. I was right in the middle of history." People were going crazy in Lisbon, she said, but when she landed in São Miguel, it was oddly quiet. Even the newspapers barely mentioned the revolution. People were cautious, as if someone was listening to everything they said.

When she went back in 1984 with her parents, she was amazed at the progress that had occurred. She hears Portugal has made great strides since then, although it still lags behind the other European

Woman standing on her balcony, Lisbon, Portugal, 1990

countries. The number of people leaving the Azores has decreased, and German, Swiss, and British immigrants are moving to the islands, reversing the trend, she said.

As a fourth generation Californian, I had no names of cousins or other living relatives to find, but I spent hours at the Civil Registry on Faial, where the young clerk combed through thirteen volumes of handwritten records looking for Anna and Manuel Souza and their son Joseph. There were many Souzas, but we didn't find names and dates that matched the information my mother had given me. However, just being where they had lived made me feel connected to them.

Even for those of us whose relatives are no longer in Portugal, there are many links to the past. It gives the heart a jolt to see your family name emblazoned on a crest painted on a cathedral ceiling or on the walls of a royal palace—Souza, Silva, Silveira, Gomes, Alves, Cabral—proof they really lived there. As the tour bus rattles past the old churches and stone villages, you can imagine what life was like for your mother, grandmother, or great-grandmother, and the stories of the old country come alive.

Despite its somber beginnings, our trip was a joyous one. Terceira is different from any place in California. As we wound through the narrow cobblestone streets, we gawked at ancient-looking stone buildings on either side. We marveled at the curious imperios, tiny red, blue, yellow, and green chapels to the Holy Ghost. We passed rock-walled pastures with giant Holstein cows, grizzled men in wool caps riding donkey carts loaded with silver milk cans, and stocky old women dressed in black from head to toe, their faces wrinkled and stubborn. Having been up all night, we were exhausted, and our heads swam in the hot, humid air, but our eyes were wide open, drinking in this new world from which our parents, grandparents, or great-grandparents had come.

Women making and selling crafts, Lisbon, Portugal, 1990

THE TIES BETWEEN the two countries today are many. The people, of course, are the strongest link. Nearly every Azorean family has friends or relatives living in the United States. An estimated $1 million in monthly American social security checks goes to people who have retired in Portugal. The Azores, Madeira, and continental Portugal are dotted with houses built with money earned in America. Asked about these houses, which are often more modern than the others around them, the guide shrugs. "Oh, those belong to the emigrants."

Portuguese youth wear American t-shirts and tennis shoes and listen to American rock and roll. The Portuguese television stations broadcast American shows with Portuguese subtitles. Although conditions have improved at home, some Portuguese still dream of moving to the United States.

The United States maintains two Air Force bases in the Azores, one on Santa Maria and one on Terceira. In July 1990, the Air Force

Band from Lackland, Texas, arrived on a whirlwind tour of the islands, and Azoreans filled the town squares to hear the tunes of Leonard Bernstein, Glenn Miller, and Portuguese American John Philip Sousa.

Californians and Azoreans blended into one happy family when a Faialese village welcomed the Dutras's tour group for dinner, music, and a craft show. It was all very familiar to the Californians, most of whom claimed family roots in Faial. They had eaten the same food—beans, *linguiça, torresmos*, yams, and sweet bread—growing up. The band played songs they had heard at Portuguese *festas* all their lives, and the crocheted doilies and dolls on the tables along the wall were the same as Mama or Grandma used to make. When it came time to dance the *chamarrita*, only their clothes separated the Americans from the Portuguese.

Portuguese women, especially those who live in the larger cities, have much in common today with their American sisters. They go to school; juggle housework, jobs, and daycare; and relax with television soap operas. However, although they are not as cloistered and restricted as they used to be, they are not as emancipated as American women. They only won full voting rights and equality under the law in 1976. Women are beginning to hold important positions in government and business, but it takes generations for change to seep through centuries of tradition.

In the Azores, you see few women on the city streets, although men lounge in front of the bars or in the city parks. The women look shyly out of the windows, pausing in their housework to watch the traffic go by. Those who venture out, especially the young women, are subject to leering looks and rude comments from the men, so they rarely go out alone, except to attend mass or to shop. Then you see them, walking quickly down the cobblestone streets, purse in one hand, plastic grocery bag in the other, hurrying to the shelter of their homes.

In the rural villages, you see the women always working, hanging clothes on the line, digging in the fields, sweeping the porches. Many old women wear the traditional widow's garb—a nunlike outfit of black dress, black stockings, and black shawl—even in very hot weather. The costume brings them respect and seems to give them more freedom.

In the big cities on Madeira and on the continent, women are important and savvy parts of the economy. You see them on street corners selling sweet bread or crocheted tablecloths. You see them in restaurants and shops catering to the tourists, and you see them at tourist attractions, hawking their souvenirs. Their traditional crafts, such as embroidery and knitting, have become big businesses, tied in with the growing tourist industry. Young women from well-to-do families study several languages in school and go to work at the big hotels or find jobs with the airlines. Others work in offices, schools, and shops, just like the California women.

Emigration from Portugal to the United States has slowed in recent years. Since the former totalitarian rule was overthrown in 1974 and a democratic government was approved in 1976, political, economic, and social conditions have improved greatly, so there is less motivation to leave. In fact, several sources report that people are immigrating to continental Portugal and the Azores in increasing numbers, attracted by the natural beauty, ancient culture, and slower pace of life. The ties across the Atlantic pull both ways. Grandma may never have gone back to Portugal, but her grandchildren did. And then they came home to California.

Glossary

Alcunha (al-COON-nya):
A nickname. In the old country, the Portuguese frequently use nicknames instead of their real names, especially when there is more than one person in a village with the same name. They might be named for an occupation, a hobby, or the way they look.

Avó (ah-VAW):
Grandmother. Only a slight change in pronunciation and punctuation makes the word *Avô*, which means grandfather.

Fado (FAH-doo):
A traditional style of singing from continental Portugal. *Fado* literally means "fate." *Fado* singing, which has been called the Portuguese blues, was originally sung for small groups of people late at night in the poor *bairros* of Lisbon. Today, *fado* singers appear in restaurants and on stage in Portugal and the United States. Accompanied by acoustic guitars, they sing of hope, hurt, longing, and love.

Feiticeira (fet-i-SAY-ra):
A witch or one who casts spells and tells fortunes.

Festa (FESH-ta):
Any festival, but especially the annual Holy Ghost festivals held in most Portuguese American communities during the spring and summer. The festivals include a mass, crowning of *festa* queens, a parade, and a feast in which *sopas*, Azorean soup, is distributed free to everyone.

Império (im-PEAR-ee-oh):
> A chapel dedicated to the Holy Ghost. In the Azores, these colorful little buildings are plentiful and serve as a focal point for the annual Holy Ghost festivals.

Linguiça (Ling-GWEE-sah):
> Portuguese sausage, especially popular among Azoreans. Traditionally, families gathered once a year to kill a pig and make *linguiça*, blood sausage, and other delicacies.

Sopas (SOOP-azh):
> An Azorean soup made of roasted beef, bread, and gravy that is one of the highlights of the annual Holy Ghost *festas*.

Bibliography

Anderson, Jean, John Bradford, and Nora O'Leary. "Portugal: Its Flavor and Its Flair." *Family Circle* June 1, 1987: 86+.

Barreno, Maria Isabel, Maria Teresa Horta, and Maria Velho da Costa. *The Three Marias: New Portuguese Letters.* New York: Doubleday & Co., 1975.

Brettell, Caroline B. "In the Absence of Men." *Natural History* Feb. 1987: 52-61.

Coelho, Art. "An American Courtship: Pumpkins at Your Door." *Portuguese Heritage Journal* Nov. 1992.

Coelho, Art. "The Azorean Immigrant: Heroic Dreamer." *Portuguese Heritage Journal* Dec. 16, 1991: 4.

Dickey, Jim. "Germana Sarmento's Life of Giving Ends at 102." *San Jose Mercury News* Sept. 2, 1992.

Emilio, Cecilia Cardoza. *Azorean Folk Customs.* San Diego: self-published, 1990.

Holmes, Lionel and Joseph D'Alessandro. *Portuguese Pioneers of the Sacramento Area.* Sacramento, CA: Portuguese Historical and Cultural Society, 1990.

Lamphere, Louise, Caroline B. Brettell, and Rita James Simon, eds. "Working Women and Family Strategies: Portuguese and Colombian Women in a New England Community." *International Migration: The Female Experience.* New Jersey: Rowman and Allanheld, 1986.

Lick, Sue Fagalde. *The Iberian Americans*. New York: Chelsea House, 1990.

Lincoln, Joseph C. *The Portygee*. New York: A.L. Burt Co., 1920.

Morgan, Robin, ed. *Sisterhood is Global*. Garden City, NY: Anchor Press, 1984.

Rogers, Francis Millet. *Atlantic Islanders of the Azores and Madeiras*. North Quincy, MA: The Christopher Publishing House, 1979.

Rogers, Francis Millet. *Americans of Portuguese Descent: A Lesson in Differentiation*. Beverley Hills, CA: Sage Publishers, 1974.

Rogers, Francis Millet. "The Portuguese Experience in the United States: Double Melt or Minority Group." *Journal of the American Portuguese Society* vol. 35: 1-14.

Simas, Mary N. "Reflections Within My Kaleidoscope." San Jose Historical Museum archives.

Simas, Mary N. "The Portuguese Dairymen of Lawrence Road." San Jose Historical Museum archives.

Smith, M. Estellie. "The Portuguese Female Immigrant: The 'Marginal Man.'" *International Migration Review* 14 (1980): 77-91.

Stonehill, Pauline Correia. *A Barrelful of Memories: Stories of My Azorean Family*. San Jose, CA: Corstone Publishing, 1995.

Van Scoy, Doris Machado. *A Quest for the Story of Antonio and Maria from the Azores to Washington Township*. Los Altos, CA: self-published, 1992.

Wolforth, Sandra K. *The Portuguese in America*. Thesis. San Jose State University, 1978.

Wood, Heather. "Sidetracks Profile: Justina Souza Uses the Past as a Springboard to the Future." *Sacramento Bee* Dec. 20, 1996.

About the Author

Sue Fagalde Lick

A SAN JOSE NATIVE, Sue Fagalde Lick traces her Portuguese roots to her mother's grandparents, who left the Azores Islands in the late 1800s. She received her bachelor's degree in journalism from San Jose State University and has over twenty-five years of newspaper and magazine experience. The author of *The Iberian Americans* (Chelsea House, 1990), she is currently working on a book about childless women and lives in Newport, Oregon.